DATE DUE	
MAY 0 9 1994 S		

Autonomy
— and —
Social Interaction

Autonomy
— and —
Social Interaction

Joseph H. Kupfer

State University of New York Press

Published by
State University of New York Press, Albany

© 1990 State University of New York

For information, address State University of New York
Press, State University Plaza, Albany, N.Y. 12246

Library of Congress Cataloging-in-Publication Data

Kupfer, Joseph H.
    Autonomy and social interaction / Joseph H. Kupfer.
    p. cm.
    ISBN 0-7914-0345-9. ——ISBN 0-7914-0346-7 (pbk.)
    1. Social interaction. 2. Autonomy (Psychology) I. Title.
HM291.K87 1990   89-27500
302—dc20   CIP

10 9 8 7 6 5 4 3 2 1

For my daughter, Gabi

Contents

Acknowledgments

I am grateful to Iowa State University for providing me with a leave of absence during which a substantial portion of this book was written.

Introduction

Autonomy has come to be a basic value, a priority in most of our lives. More than such established goods as happiness, ·virtue, and knowledge, it has become a crux of debate in both personal and political arenas. Disputes about work, education, child-rearing, and spousal conduct typically turn on considerations of autonomy. And in the political sphere, concerns over civil rights, abortion, and economic exploitation are fought out in terms of autonomy. Perhaps this is because autonomy occupies a foundational place among our many and varied values. Whether we value something, choose to pursue it, or critically assess its subsequent experience, largely depends upon our degree of autonomy. Without autonomy we can't decide whether what we value is worth cherishing or pursuing; we can't plan to become one sort of person rather than another. In this respect, then, the question of autonomy may be said to underlie other goods. We can always ask of any value whether it is held or sought in an autonomous fashion.

Nevertheless, it is good to remember that autonomy is a distinctively Western value and one that has emerged only in the last few hundred years of "Modern" philosophy and commitment. Nietzsche wrote that man is the "unfinished animal." The question then is, "How shall man be finished?" The emerging Modern ("autonomian") view answers that man must finish himself rather than be defined by an external authority. The project of self-completion presupposes autonomy—developed capacities for self-determination as well as freedom from interference. Let's consider freedom from interference or restraint "liberty." It entails having options for choice and action.

Liberty is needed both to acquire and exercise autonomy, but autonomy is not liberty and requires more than liberty for its development and deployment. We could exercise the options afforded by liberty in a non-autonomous way: acting on ideas and values borrowed uncritically from others or doing what others tell us to do. We might realize an opportunity which we are at liberty to enjoy in a merely conventional or habitual way.[1] Moreover, we can fail altogether to avail ourselves of opportunities that exist due to lack of autonomy. Because of dependence on another or inability to control our emotions, for example, we might be unable to see or seize an opportunity.

The autonomous person's beliefs, values, and actions are somehow his "own." He determines his own ends and sets his own course of conduct. Autonomous choices and actions express the individual's preferences and aspirations. This requires conditions for developing independence of thought, the capacity for critical evaluation, strength of will, and confidence in one's ability to plan and carry out action. Liberty without this sort of autonomy is without value. Options without the ability to act on them independently are of no significance to the individual in question. They are like the chance to buy what we can't afford or enjoy what we can't appreciate—so many mirages of possible experience.

Because autonomy has not been recognized, much less valued, until fairly recently, it is easy to see it as historically determined or conditioned and so lacking in what might be considered "transcendental" importance. I'm not going to quarrel directly with those who take such a view, though the second chapter (on respect) indirectly addresses this by arguing for the value of autonomy. I will confront those who underestimate the significance of autonomy or lament it as merely a symptom of twentieth-century anomie. One who formidably does both is Alisdair MacIntyre in *After Virtue*. Bemoaning the lack of a unifying tradition in our age, MacIntyre sees moral theory and discourse as fragmented (so far, so good). The contemporary emphasis on freedom or autonomy is but a further symptom of this lack of tradition to give unity to our moral thought. For MacIntyre, freedom is the calling card of an individualism which stresses the satisfaction of private desires at the expense of social meaning.

Although he offers a profound historico-cultural diagnosis of contemporary dilemmas and quandaries, MacIntyre's own solution is a tip-off to his major weakness. He languishes in a nostalgic call for preserving the Scholastic virtues until the collapse of modern morality makes their resurrection feasible. We must keep the flame of some past tradition burning amidst the chaos of rootless moralizing. What MacIntyre fails to see is that a new tradition is underway. Since Hobbes and Kant, Western culture has been moving toward a conception of autonomy as a foundational value. The Hobbesian strand of this movement conceives of freedom as liberty. It is a political perspective which understands the good life as maximal satisfaction of our desires with minimal interference by others or government. It is this impoverished and impoverishing conception of freedom that I think MacIntyre is justified in despairing over.

But another strand of modern thinking, descended from Kant and Rousseau, understands freedom as self-legislation. For Kant, this is individualistic and interior, consisting of the rational formulation of and adherence to moral principles. As we shall see in chapter 1, this is too narrow both in its moralistic content and in ignoring the material context of lived life. Rousseau conceives of freedom within the context of community. The struggle of this approach is to integrate the individual within the social whole *without* a definitive tradition and *with* his freedom intact. For Rousseau, this requires a commitment to and explication of legitimate political process. Rousseau's project, unlike the one undertaken in this book, is essentially political. He is concerned with reconciling individual freedom with legitimate political authority so that the individual can be obliged to obey the state and still be free.

The more general tension for champions of autonomy is between individual freedom and social integration. To me, the ideal seems to be autonomous individuals living in community, developing traditions and institutions which confer enriching identities on their members. This is what Marx considered "concrete individuality," in which the individual's autonomy is harmonized, even enhanced, within a socioeconomic framework. The two deficient extremes are more easily achieved than is this harmony of autonomy and community.

At one pole, autonomy degenerates into mere "subjective" freedom: an alienated, self-contained individual bereft of collective, social life. She achieves independence at the expense of the shared meaning which communal ties and organizations provide. This is caricatured by the image of the contemporary Yuppie—well-off, fashionable, unfettered by tradition, at liberty to consume commodities, but with no communal context to sustain her. Without community, autonomy tends toward self-absorption and alienation. This suggests that autonomy is not sufficient for the good life. We might say, paraphrasing Kant, that autonomy without community is empty; it lacks the content needed to make life complete. On the other hand (at the other extreme), without autonomy, community is likely to be stultifying.

The bonds of community threaten to restrict people in their quest for what they take to be best for them. Traditions and traditional values often smother talents and energies that could actually further the community's ends. We have only to note the millenia-long subjugation of women to see the truth of this. What's gained, of course, is the sort of stability which doesn't issue from autonomously resolved conflicts and tensions. This species of unity is not very feasible for us. For one thing, the ideal of autonomy, if not its actuality, is too prevalent in American society (as well as a growing portion of the rest of the world). For another, the cost is great in terms of individual growth and happiness. We might say, continuing our Kantian paraphrase, that community without autonomy is blind. It lacks the guidance and direction and vision which autonomous people supply.

Lawrence Haworth puts the case more strongly: "A community, one may say, just by virtue of being a community, has no value whatever."[2] The shared way of life and purposes of the community must themselves be good. Haworth asks us to consider a community of Nazis or automatons. And this is instructive. However, he sees autonomy and only autonomy, as giving value to community. While I concur that autonomy adds value, and may be necessary for the fullest life possible within community, I think his position is too strong. A community can have many values even as it limits people's autonomy (sometimes because it limits their autonomy).

A community may be enriched by other important values such as kindness, love, and happiness. A community of Quakers, Mennonites, or monks might have little autonomy but still promote human flourishing. I agree with Haworth that it wouldn't be complete flourishing, but then partial flourishing is also likely in a community of autonomous individuals. Perhaps we can tentatively leave it that a community of autonomous individuals, in principle, has more potential for the good life and is not by its very structure cut off from avenues of human fulfillment.

The ideal is for our relationships with others to foster the autonomy of those involved, for our interactions to develop our capacities for self-governance and widen our range of choice. I have no comprehensive schema for creating an autonomous society. Rather, my much more modest undertaking is to investigate several specific relationships and contexts of interaction in which autonomy is pivotal.

I will look at the reciprocity between autonomy and social interactions from both sides: examining the role of autonomy in these interactions, and investigating the way our interactions in turn shape autonomy. The first involves showing the relevance and importance of autonomy for these social relationships. Autonomy grounds specific conduct and considerations. For example, an individual's ability to function autonomously may require that we refrain from lying to him. However, the fact that someone has restricted our autonomy, or threatens to do so, may excuse or even justify our lying to him. Autonomy also conditions certain relationships, such as that between parents and children. Whether or not children autonomously accept benefits from their parents is germane to whether they are obliged to reciprocate. And inequality in autonomy vis-a-vis their parents is an obstacle to adult children becoming their friends.

On the other hand, autonomy is promoted or limited, developed or truncated, by virtue of our interactions with others. Privacy, for example, is essential to the development of the sort of self-concept needed for autonomous living. In order for an individual to develop a conception of himself as an independent originator of thought and action, he must enjoy periods of independence from interference and observation. Mirroring the private is the public domain of architecture; built space can frustrate or foster autonomy in several ways. Buildings structure choice and control over what we see and do, help mold our body-image, and determine the nature and extent of our social interaction.

With a subject as broad as autonomy, selection of topics is to some extent arbitrary, reflecting the author's keenest interests. Although no doubt true here, there is a rationale governing what has been omitted. This is a work in social philosophy, concerned with the way autonomy figures in various social contexts. The scope of those contexts has been limited by concentrating on non-institutional interactions and relations. I try to confine my examination of autonomy to areas of life which do not involve highly systematized or regulated organizations of people. In order to provide focus and depth, institutionalized power structures are not dealt with directly. Thus, various institutional arrangements which seriously bear on autonomy are omitted: science, medicine, education, law, government, and economy—to mention the more conspicuous.

Autonomy is relevant to and enmeshed in every facet of life. The workplace, for example, is a prime locus of issues of autonomy. Indeed, it could further situate the discussions of lying, privacy, and respect. But, to investigate the workplace would naturally take us into issues of institutionalized power, thence to larger considerations of capitalism and socialism, and the whole wide world of political economics. This clearly would take us too far afield. So, I try to deal with autonomy in relations that are social but not "societal," in the sense of institutionalized power structures.

The broad canvas of morality is similarly narrowed. Taking up autonomy from a social perspective means engaging moral matters in light of human interactions and relationships. Moral obligation and character, for instance, are dealt with in the discussions of privacy and the parent-child relationship. But the social dynamic of that practice and relationship, the interpersonal stakes and stances, are emphasized rather than the precise lineaments of moral goodness and badness, rights or obligations. I don't, therefore, go into the difference between legal, political, and moral rights in the parent-child relationship. An autonomy-oriented approach is primarily concerned with the effect of relations and actions on autonomy and how autonomy in turn should determine social relations. This includes how autonomy bears on questions of obligation and responsibility. I look at obligation and responsibility in light of autonomic considerations, only to the extent that autonomy is implicated.

I will examine respect in a similar light. Considerations of autonomy impose obligation of respect. Autonomy is the ground of respectful consideration owed people. The ability of people to function autonomously imposes constraints and demands upon our behavior. Such considerations are further defined in particular contexts of interaction, such as the parent-child relationship and the opportunity for lying. In the former, the goal of promoting autonomy obliges certain behavior of parents because of their both priviliged and responsible relationship to the children. In the matter of lying, our obligation to refrain from lying is articulated in terms of the curtailment of the liar's as well as the deceived's autonomy.

The book is written to be read either as an integrated treatment of autonomy or as a series of self-sufficient analyses of independent issues. As a whole it provides an ongoing examination of the nature of autonomy and how it plays a central role in social relationships. The chapter on respect pursues the more abstract analysis of autonomy begun in the first chapter by articulating the broad demands autonomy makes on our interactions with others. Those demands are further specified in the examination of the liar-deceived interaction. We then see how autonomy informs the parent-child relationship. The discussion picks up the themes of respect and obligation in this particular relationship and goes on to show how autonomy helps define it. Since privacy is necessary to the child developing the sort of self-concept ingredient in autonomous functioning, the chapter on privacy helps fill in this portrait. Finally, we see how the public role of architecture complements privacy as a pervasive determinant of autonomy.

These last two chapters, it should be noted, include causal claims about the social conditions under which autonomy develops and flourishes. For support of these empirical claims, I refer to studies and theorizing by sociologists and psychologists. It seems appropriate that investigations in moral psychology and philosophical anthropology be buttressed by the work of social scientists.

Various topics also fit together in sub-groups: lying as a specific mode of failure to respect other and self; privacy as a fundamental way we show respect for one another in general, and in the parent-child relationship in particular; architecture as the public medium of the autonomy nurtured by the opportunity for privacy. Key themes run through different chapters, such as the nature of dependency, self-concept and knowledge, personal identity, and authority. At the same time, each chapter can stand fairly well on its own. Those wishing to pursue one or more topics in their own right can readily do so.

The goal of the approach taken here is to reveal how autonomy is a basic moral value, woven through different spheres of daily, social life. Seeing how it figures in a range of social relationships should deepen our understanding of autonomy and at the same time shed light on these relationships.

CHAPTER ONE

Autonomy:
Dimensions and Distinctions,
Conditions and Constraints

Autonomy is a complex concept and topic. Recent discussions reveal different types, levels, conditions for, and limits on it. Consequently, the purpose of this chapter is to draw together these sundry conceptions and discussions, if only in the process to clarify different aspects of autonomy.

I will begin by distinguishing between intellectual and volitional autonomy. Next, I will demarcate its moral and nonmoral domains, as well as the first and second-order exercise of autonomy. In the course of examining these aspects of autonomy, I shall also discuss obstacles to or constraints on its exercise, and their different sources. However, I will mention only their correlates—conditions which make possible or enlarge autonomy. This is because later chapters will analyze these conditions in considerable depth. The personal, social, and physical relationships which enable us to function autonomously will be examined, for example, in chapters on privacy, the parent-child relationship, and architecture. Hence, for now, I will concentrate on the obstacles to autonomy as its various dimensions are delineated.

Autonomy is self-determination. The autonomous person is one who chooses for himself what to think and what to do. He is self-governing in that his actions spring from interests and values that he has in some sense decided upon. Moreover, his beliefs are arrived at independently, by means of critical reasoning. In his beliefs and actions, then, the autonomous individual is guided by his own notion of what is right or best, feasible or desirable. Particular decisions may ultimately be based on his conception of the sort of person he thinks he ought to become, or life he thinks worth living.

As this tentative description suggests, the autonomous individual has a mind and will of his own. For a start, then, we do well to distinguish between autonomy of judgment and volitional autonomy. To speak of an individual functioning autonomously is imprecise and could refer to either or both human abilities. The individual must be able to think critically about his beliefs and values. This includes assessing the justification for these beliefs and reflecting on his epistemic standards. In addition, autonomy of will is needed to make plans and weigh the relative importance of different goals. Deliberating over choices, arriving at decisions, and finally acting on them, requires autonomy of will. Let's first consider intellectual autonomy, the autonomy of judgement.

Autonomy of Judgment

Autonomy in judgment is "thinking for oneself." It is a matter of forming beliefs on the basis of evidence, reasoning from similar cases, and anticipating contingencies as well as estimating their likelihood. The individual must also apply epistemic standards. Recourse to standards is necessary in order to assess the strength of evidence, the consistency of beliefs, and the quality of arguments. The fully autonomous individual, moreover, holds these standards critically, aware of their limits and value. He is, for instance, wary when he reads studies which report correlations between variables. He appreciates that without such constraints as control groups, correlations have but limited implications.

In its typical exercise, intellectual autonomy involves an awareness of how beliefs are justified, by both first-hand investigations as well as reliable testimony. Since it would be impractical to directly ascertain the truth of most of our beliefs, a good deal of intellectual autonomy turns upon assessing the testimony of others. This requires that we possess "criteria of reliability," criteria by which to recognize an authority or when someone's testimony is dependable. We have to be able to tell when the speaker has access to truth through direct knowledge or access to still another's findings. As John Benson notes, the value of this autonomy in judgment is that it maximizes one's chances of having justified true beliefs.[1]

To exercise intellectual autonomy in this assessment of epistemic justification, the capacities which broadly define "intelligence" or "reason" must be developed. John Dewey elaborates on this theme in the following way:

> Reason as a noun signifies the happy cooperation of a multitude of dispositions, such as sympathy, curiosity, exploration, experimentation, frankness, pursuit—to follow things through—circumspection, to look about at the context, etc.,. . ."[2]

It is important to bear these diverse dispositions in mind lest we think that autonomy of judgment requires simply turning the pure light of an abstract intellect on the world. Indeed, Benson sees autonomy of judgement itself as dispositional: the proper degree and kind of reliance on both self and others. As such it is a mean between two extremes. An excess of self-reliance yields, "arrogant self-sufficiency," in which the individual foolishly relies on his own judgment rather than another's.[3] The deficiency consists in depending too much on the support, prompting, and advice of others. Such a person accepts what he is told with little or no (good) reason to think the testimony reliable.

Clearly, this means that autonomy of judgment requires a sort of practical wisdom: the ability to judge when someone else knows better than oneself. And this involves both judging one's own limits and strengths as well as those of others. Without this critical intellectual skill the individual is doomed to err on the side of either too little or too much reliance on others (or both, at different times!). It seems reasonable to say, therefore, that autonomy of judgment depends upon self-knowledge, as well as a certain sort of, perhaps unteachable, acumen.

With the idea of dependence, we come to the matter of constraints or limitations on autonomy of judgment. It will be helpful to make a provisional distinction between internal and external constraints. External constraints typically interfere with the exercise of autonomy, as with deception or censorship. They either suggest spurious possibilities which misdirect the individual's thinking or keep her ignorant of pertinent information. More radical interferences with intellectual autonomy are brainwashing, aversion therapy, and lobotomy. They are more radical in that they alter the thought processes themselves rather than mislead them or supply them with spoiled goods.

Internal restrictions are due to some condition suffered by the individual rather than outside interference. Typically, they will consist in deficiencies or "defects" in rationality. The abilities which make up judgment or intelligence can be limited, for instance, by mental retardation or severe emotional disturbance. Mental disorders, such as paranoia, also limit autonomy by impairing judgment. The paranoic has a belief structure which provides him with only fantasy-options. He has so fabricated his own world that no testimony or evidence counts against his beliefs. "The paranoic adopts cognitive strategies that isolate him from counter-evidence, and so deprives himself of the distinction between phantasy and reality."[4]

Let us return to dependence, the constraint on autonomy of judgment with which we broached the topic. The dependent person accepts what he's told with little or no reason to think the testimony reliable. He is not himself able to justify those beliefs which issue from his dependency. On the face of it, dependence on another's intellect and belief would seem to be an external limit. The dependent individual is less autonomous because he relies on something external to himself—another person. Construing dependence as an extternal restriction is apt when the dependence is a result of the other's interference, as with manipulation of the dependent person. However, the dependent relationship may arise because of the dependent person's unwitting habituation, weakness, or even choice. The dependence might also be the result of some combination of external interference and internal weakness, as in some cases of adult children relying too much on their parents. It might be best to construe dependence, then, as a relational restriction on autonomy of judgment: a constraint on autonomy constituted by the relation between the individual and another.

As this brief discussion of dependence may have suggested, external and internal limits on autonomy can "cooperate," or one can beget the other. Although usually an external restriction on autonomy of will, economic deprivation can also indirectly produce internal limits on autonomy of judgment. By greatly reducing an individual's cultural and educational experience, poverty (an external constraint) can issue in restricted intellectual abilities and dispositions. Not only might the individual lack such skills as reading, analysis, or deduction in a significant degree, but he could also lack the very disposition to inquire and criticize. The joys of the life of the intellect may escape him with the result that he takes little delight in exercising the abilities in which reason consists. The upshot is a curtailment in autonomy of judgment from within, but it is the product of the external condition of poverty. Conversely, adequate economic wherewithal provides at least the opportunity for autonomous functioning.

Autonomy of judgment is distinct from autonomy of will. But level of autonomy in intellectual functioning will obviously affect the scope and degree of an individual's autonomy of will. The exercise of a wide range of intellectual abilities is needed to assess possible courses of action, for example. Moreover, cognitive abilities are needed to evaluate particular choices as well as the mode of choosing after the decision is made and the action performed. This amounts to the ability to examine and evaluate the exercise of autonomy (of both judgment and volition) itself. Constraints on autonomy of judgment must impede autonomy of will. Because a retarded person's intellectual abilities are limited, for instance, his range and degree of autonomy of will are correspondingly limited.

While autonomy of judgment is no doubt necessary for autonomous deliberation and action, it is not sufficient. Because of either external or internal conditions the individual may be incapable of acting or even choosing in accordance with his freely made judgment. This brings us to autonomy of will and the ways in which it is frustrated or limited.

Autonomy of Will

Autonomy of will can be divided into two spheres of exercise. *Efficacy* of will indicates the ability to do what one wills. *Deliberateness* of will refers to the extent to which what it is that one wills is the fruit of deliberate choice. The first sphere is "executive," while the second is "judicial/legislative." The former concerns putting one's will into action; the latter, determining what should be willed in the first place.

A. *Efficacy of Will*

Efficacy of will might more colloquially be called autonomy of action, since it refers to our ability to act on our decisions or will. Obviously, it requires certain resources, skills, and freedom from obstruction. If one wants to play the piano but has no access to the instrument, her will lacks efficacy. On the other hand, receiving instruction at an early age clearly enhances this sphere of one's autonomy. The ability to do what one wills is also dependent on the sort of person one is, on whether or not one is disciplined, perservering, tenacious. This is because both the world and one's other desires or emotions can impede the execution of one's will. Let's examine efficacy of will more fully by taking up external, internal, and relational restrictions on it.

It is easy to see how autonomy of action can be interfered with. Interference can range from physical limitation to coercion or exploitation. The latter limit the individual by, "attaching costs to certain forms of action that they would not otherwise carry."[5] Although threats and exploitative demands work through the individual's thought processes, they do not actually limit her autonomy of judgment. Rather, they limit her choice of action by means of alternatives presented for her to judge. Closely related are situations in which we restrict someone's autonomy of action by restricting her autonomy of judgment.

Because someone believes a lie, for instance, the limitation on her thinking in turn limits her range of action. By suggesting possibilities which are not really there or foreclosing on live options, the lie prompts the deceived to pursue what can't be had or discourages her from pursuing what is within reach. Similarly, censorship deprives people of information; when unaware of options, people can't intentionally pursue them. In these sorts of case, interference with autonomy of judgment mediates the interference with autonomy of action.

External constraints on efficacy of will may not be interferences so much as deprivations. Poverty limits what one is able to do by making certain courses of action impossible. Various opportunities are restricted, from what work is available to what interests may be pursued and environments enjoyed. Poverty can also limit the efficacy of will indirectly by limiting autonomy of judgment. The autonomy of judgment of poor people is often limited by lack of information and meagerness of education. Thus intellectually restricted, the poor are unable to do all sorts of beneficial things.

On the other hand, our relationships with others can just as obviously enhance or even make possible autonomy of action. Other people can bring possibilities to our attention as well as facilitate the realization of our goals. On a still deeper level, others, such as parents and friends, can help us develop the very abilities needed for autonomous action. These include such strengths as the ability to foresee the implications of our conduct, sensitivity to changes in surroundings, ability to imagine alternatives among our options, and fortitude to see a plan of action through.

Because efficacy of will requires various psychological strengths and skills, their lack poses an internal threat to this sphere of autonomy. Thus, an individual can lack autonomy of action because of some psychological defect or disorder. Stanley Benn's example of the psychopath nicely illustrates how someone could have autonomy of judgment but lack autonomy of action. Psychopaths cannot carry through projects requiring deferment of gratification. Only immediate consequences of action count as relevant considerations for decision-making.

> In appreciating the nature of the alternatives he may exhibit quite a high degree of epistemic rationality [autonomy of judgment]. But he will be attracted to one rather than another only by the expectation of greater immediate gratification. Though he may grasp that disastrous results will certainly follow, this does not move him.[6]

As with internal impediments to autonomy of *judgment,* there are less dramatic internal deficiencies which limit autonomy of action; namely, those which constitute old-fashioned "weakness of will." This occurs when we fail to do what we belive to be the "best" thing, and doing so is within our power. Strength of will is needed to resist the pull of immediate preferences or desires which run counter to what we judge to be a preferable course of conduct. As Robert Ladenson points out, moreover, the hindrance to doing what we will isn't always an opposing desire.

> Emotions such as anger, fear, envy, etc., and habits such as laziness, self-pity, defeatism, and so forth, can all cause a person to act in ways that he recognizes to be unintelligent [not doing what is deemed best] in restrospect or even at the time.[7]

Put positively, efficacy of will depends on what Robert Roberts calls "virtues of will power," those virtues which manage our desires and aversions. "We can be more and less 'good at' breaking bad habits and forming new ones, at 'deferring gratification,' at resisting cravings and impulses. . ."[8] Efforts of will are made by means of such virtues as patience, courage, and self-control. Thus, we can look at weakness of will as referring to the presence of some things: unruly desires, obstructing passions, and debilitating habits. Or, we can look at it as the absence of the very virtues which enable us to carry out our will.

Strength and weakness of will make no reference to the justification of one's beliefs. That would rather be a matter of judgment. Consequently, a person could have a strong will and make poor choices, perhaps because of defects in judgment. Conversely, a weak-willed individual could aim, albeit fruitlessly, at the truly best goals and means to their achievement.

The last sort of constraint on efficacy of will or autonomy of action is relational in nature. One such relation also involves weakness of will. When external conditions make realizing our will difficult, it may not be accurate simply to label the restriction external. Sometimes it isn't just the external obstacles which restrict an individual. Strength of will is needed to overcome external obstacles as well as internal ones and someone with discipline and patience may be able to succeed where a weaker person is thwarted. Where a reasonable amount of willpower could overcome the obstacle, it seems plausible to think of the constraint on autonomy of action as relational: involving the interplay between the external hindrance and the individual's weakness of will.

An individual can also lack autonomy of action by being dependent on others to do what he should be doing for himself. This, too, may be mediated by a lack of autonomy in judgment, as when the individual depends on others to weigh evidence, make evaluations, and draw conclusions which the individual should be weighing, making, and drawing for himself. However, the "action dependence" can be more immediate, involving dependence on others to carry out the individual's requests and to meet his needs. Sometimes the dependent person manipulates others to do these things for him. This clouds the issue of dependence, since manipulators need not be dependent in the sense of having their autonomy restricted, but rather use their manipulative skills to augment their autonomy. However, when the manipulator can no longer do these things for himself because his abilities to carry out his will have atrophied, then what perhaps began as clever contrivance has become dependence.

As remarked earlier, autonomy of judgment obviously contributes to autonomy of action. The person who is able to evaluate his beliefs free from interference with the needed information at his disposal, clearly has greater scope for acting. But the reverse is also true, if less obvious; autonomy of action can further autonomy of judgment. Autonomy of action enables us to "test" our beliefs by acting on them and noticing the consequences of so doing. The success or failure of our actions in securing anticipated results is crucial to assessing the warrant of our beliefs. The more autonomous we are in our actions, the greater the opportunity to evaluate beliefs, as well as the procedures used to justify them. In addition, if this yields greater ability to observe, predict, and draw inferences, then we have that much more autonomy of judgment because of our autonomy of action.

This concludes my discussion of efficacy of will and the restrictions on it. We have seen that efficacy of will involves the ability to do what one wills, the constraints on which may be external, internal, or relational. Autonomy of will has another dimension, that of deliberateness, to which I now turn.

B. Deliberateness of Will[9]

The nature of one's will is relevant to the question of autonomy. Depending on why one wills what one does, or how the will is formed, it may be more or less autonomous. What one wills may be determined exclusively or predominantly by the strength of one's desires and impulses. Such a person then acts or makes an attempt to act solely in accordance with his strongest prompting. If he is both hungry and tired, he will eat if his hunger is greater than his fatigue and vice versa. This sort of will consists of the most demanding, urgent force within the individual. It need not be an "immediate" desire, in the sense of being temporally proximate. It could be the desire for something quite distant such as wealth, revenge, or professional advancement. But it will be an "immediate" desire in that its force will be felt in the present, at the time of the willing.

Such a will is in some sense less one's own, hence less autonomous, than it might be. The individual whose will is determined solely by the intensity of his desires and aversions is but the "playground for different forces."[10] This is to say that the individual himself is not determining his will so much as having it determined for him, albeit by components of his self. This is a version of a Platonic theme: that such a person is ruled by his desires, under their domination, rather than in control of his own life. The alternative of deliberating, then, gives an individual self-mastery, and with it, greater autonomy of will.

This non-deliberative person, pushed and pulled by his desires, is labeled by Harry Frankfurt a "wanton." A wanton is someone who is not "concerned with whether the desires which move him to act are desires by which he wants to be moved to act."[11] Although his desires move him to act, he does not prefer or choose to be moved by those desires. Frankfurt sees this as ignoring the question of what his will is to be. What sort of deliberation is missing from such a person, or from any of us when on occasion we behave "wantonly?" Clearly, even the wanton has to give minimal thought to the means by which to satisfy his desires. So, the deliberation missing must concern the objectives, the aims of these desires and not merely alternatives to their satisfaction.

The sort of deliberation definitive of autonomy of will involves assessing our preferences, evaluating the worth-whileness of our desires, and finally arriving at some ordering of them. This seems essential for the self-mastery in which the individual orders desires in terms of their importance, their value rather than by some aspect of their quantity, such as intensity, duration, or urgency.[12] Rather than have the desires claim our interest or command our involvment, "We try not to. . . have our place in our situation wholly structured by them [desires], but to retain our self-possession, our power to order them and not they us."[13] Dent agrees with Eschete in emphasizing the judgment of the importance of an objective or end. It is this "cool" rational reflection together with the decision to rank our preferences in a certain way that makes us masters of our desires instead of subordinate to them.

Reaching a judgment about what is best to do in the circumstances includes considering, "the merits and demerits of the possible alternative courses of action which are available," as well as the reasons for or against the various possibilities.[14] In doing so, the strength or urgency of a particular desire can very well be taken into account—as but one consideration to be weighed against others. Consequently, the individual, "may decide that he would secure peace of mind and freedom from an insistent unsatisfied longing if he were to gratify an intense desire that he feels."[15] But, as Dent rightly goes on to point out, the intensity of the desire does not rule out other courses of action. Rather, it is the individual's judgment that all things considered, it is best to satisfy the (intense) desire now. If the individual thinks that what he longs for is actually bad, then he might choose to endure it or seek some form of distraction from it.

It is precisely because we can and do attach varying degrees of significance to the objects of our desires and passions that we have a basis for denying some of them their object. We are able to see some concerns or interests as excessive or distorted only because we have put them in a larger, evaluative context. In addition, when we have evaluated the significance of something, made it important, it motivates us. This is to say that the prospect of attaining something can move us because we deem it important (rather than deeming it important because it moves us). This is similar to the Platonic reversal of pleasure and the good. Where the hedonist claims that something is deemed good because it is pleasant, Plato proposes that, for some of us anyway, something gives pleasure because it is good.

To make judgments, some degree of ordering of desires and goals is required. Typically, the ordering is piecemeal, not taking a vast array of interests into account—perhaps confined by the matter at hand or some already decided upon objective, such as restoring one's health. But whatever the degree of the ordering, the judgments of importance must be "personal," involving personal commitment to seek what is held valuable.[16] It isn't enough that the individual view an objective as worthwhile in the abstract, as in: "It's good for people to have close friends." Rather, she must see at as her good and determine upon pursuing it. Eschete sees this ranking of desires as what makes them "one's own." Consequently, a person is free if he is acting out of a desire of his own, one that he has evaluated and decided to act on. Actions springing from higher priority desires more fully express the self.

Therefore, when there is a conflict between a desire judged important and one considered trivial, should the agent act out of the less important one, frustrating the more valued, he is unfree in that action. Why? Because, as Eschete puts it, he has subordinated his self (here defined by his central desires) to what is peripheral.[17] I should add that such unfreedom is akin to if not identical with weakness of will.

There is yet a higher level at which our deliberations may proceed. We can assess and make decisions about who we are and what we wish to become. We can take up the question of what sort of person to be and what kind of life to lead. This sort of deliberation goes beyond the ordering of priorities. It addresses the nature of the self and the extent to which the individual purposely chooses to be this sort of person rather than that sort. Although on a continuum with other facets of deliberateness of the will, this self-evaluation and self-forming occupies a distinct topic in discussions of autonomy. Indeed, some philosophers go so far as to identify autonomy with second-order judgments, decisions, and desires. We will postpone discussion of it, therefore, until we consider first and second-order autonomy.

It may be worth noting here how deliberateness of will and autonomy of action (efficacy of will) are mutually supportive. In the first place, without autonomy of action there would hardly be any point in deliberating about one's desires; they would either be satisfied or not—depending upon circumstances beyond one's control. In the second place, autonomy of action is needed to assess our deliberate ordering of desires and interests. We may think that work really matters more to us than raising a family until we act on this conviction. By acting on our evaluations of desires and passions (and then exercising autonomy of judgment) we have them confirmed or give ourselves the opportunity to revise their ranking.

On the other hand, deliberateness of will may be needed for autonomy of action. Imagine someone whose desires are of equal strength and in conflict. Each desire presents an obstacle to another since its satisfaction requires frustrating another. Because this person is "at war with himself,"[18] his autonomy of action is stymied. The deliberate ordering of his desires would seem essential to establishing autonomy of action. Even such internal obstacles as compulsions and weakness of will can sometimes be meliorated by a combination of deliberative ordering and the sort of self-reflection which bespeaks autonomy of judgment.

This last observation points to a fact in our everyday experience. In our ordinary affairs we rarely need to distinguish between autonomy of judgment and autonomy of the will. Only in aberrant or extreme cases are we autonomous or not *qua* one who judges or wills. The distinction is most needed and helpful in dealing with the untoward, for instance, in matters of restrictions on autonomy. Typically, then, we deal with the overall autonomy of the whole individual. In this spirit, the spirit of our ordinary affairs, I'd like to push a little further in characterizing autonomy; in particular, by examining the habits and dispositions and their relations, which give us greater scope in both judging and willing.

The Habits of Autonomy

The tie between autonomy of judgment and autonomy of will is strong. However, there is yet another consideration which suggests that the distinction itself is somewhat artificially drawn. In the lives of real people, various habits, emotions, and their combination, span the judgment-action dichotomy. Far-reaching features of character and personality so integrate thought and action, judging and willing, that it is only in reflection, for purposes of analysis, that they can or should be distinguished.

Certain habits coordinate perceptions, emotions, and thoughts so as to dispose us to particular behavior. Kindness, for instance, involves the habits of perceiving need, sympathizing with it, and acting to meliorate it. It creates specific expectations, discriminates among features in our surroundings, and prepares us to respond to particular situations in determinate ways. Still other habits apply directly to both thought and action: perseverance and procrastination, for example. These sorts of tendencies are rarely confined to the sphere of just thought or action. Instead, they encompass both. Perhaps because thinking is a type of activity, people who tend to persevere in thinking are disposed to see a course of action through; while those who procrastinate in action tend to put off thinking out demanding scenarios.

Attentiveness and imagination also seem to be generalizable strengths, generalizable across different contexts and between thought and action. Attentiveness can help us to see and act on what is important as well as to notice crucial aspects of our own thinking processes. Imagination also spans our thinking and acting. A rich imagination enables us to propose diverse hypotheses, explanations, and even ways of reasoning. Similarly, the reach of our imagination can ferret out possibilities for action and the satisfaction of our interests. We will reconsider the pivotal role of imagination shortly.

The sorts of mutuality, overlap, and integration which characterize thought and action don't vitiate the distinction, a distinction which we have seen to be workable in getting clear on hindrances to autonomy. They do suggest that the distinction cuts into what is "naturally" a continuous thread of autonomy or its lack.

What I want to zero in on is the way "overall" autonomy is strengthened through flexibility: the ability to respond creatively and constructively to a variety of circumstances; this includes the ability to adapt to change. It results from the integration of numerous, diverse habits. John Dewey contrasts the development of a chicken's abilities to that of a human's. The chick, which can peck accurately at food shortly after hatching, quickly develops its expertise in behavior because it stems from only a few original tendencies. Its immediate efficiency, however, is "like a railway ticket, . . . good for one route only." Whereas, "A being who, in order to use his eyes, ears, hands, and legs, has to experiment in making varied combinations of their reactions, achieves a control that is flexible and varied."[19] What Dewey says here about motor skills holds equally for habits of thought and perception, emotional and social response.

Coordinating many habits that tug in different directions gives the individual greater autonomy in future thought and action. Each of the integrated habits is "freed" to re-enter new relationships with other habits. This is because integration involves varied combinations of numerous, diverse habits. Because a given habit is coordinated with many different other habits, it is not cemented into a narrow pattern. It does not become rigid in its operation. Tied to no narrow set of other habits, this habit is "free" to form various combinations, depending on the circumstances.

The habit of observing, for instance, is freed for further tie-ins as a result of combining with different habits and interests in microscope work, game hunting, social gatherings, basketball playing, and aviation. It is like using the same muscles to play a variety of sports. The individual does not get muscle-bound because each set of muscles is disposed to align in different ways with other muscle groups.

Now this process of integrating habits and interests is itself subject to scrutiny. We can develop meta-habits for reflecting on the tendencies of habit-development. Some people are better able to combine diverse habits because they have better develped those "master habits" of self-observation and projection. As Dewey notes, there are ". . . habits which experience has shown to make us sensitive, generous, imaginative, impartial in perceiving the tendency of our . . . activities."[20] These habits enable us to grasp the nature of the first-order habits and dispositions which direct our daily activities. First-order habits have objective features, just as chemical elements do. And like a good scientist, we can glean these features from experience and consciously set about integrating them in numerous and varied combinations.

Among such meta-habits are those which constitute a vivid practical imagination, one that is able to project lines of action involving subtle and far-reaching connections among habits and interests. Such an imagination envisions the way particular choices integrate or frustrate the combining of first-order habits and interests. Our ability to improvise in the face of the unforeseen stems from habits that are recombinable upon the promptings of an imagination that itself is flexible. So, even on the meta-level of the second-order habits which enable our imaginative portrayal of everyday habits in their relations, even there flexibility is crucial. Even there it is achieved through the integration of numerous and varied habits. A flexible imagination combines habits of memory, sorting, projecting, and choosing. An imagination so formed is able to foresee the impact on us of possible courses of action. We picture how a particular career or spouse is likely to affect us, including its impact on our imagination itself. Isn't this just the danger of certain occupations, that they groove our habits of imagination, narrowing our capacities for imaginatively rehearsing a variety of scenarios, including those which shape who we will become.[21]

My suggestion here is that the flexibility which comes from the integration of varied and numerous habits, on both the everyday and second-order level, increases our autonomy of judgement and will.

First and Second-Order, Moral and Non-Moral

In what follows, our concern will be with choice, decision, and selfhood. Sometime autonomy of judgment will figure more importantly, sometimes autonomy of will (usually, deliberateness). In most cases, both will enter in. Usually, then, we will be treating autonomy integrally, as one thing. It can be variously employed in both moral and non-moral matters, and in first-order and second-order decisions. Consequently, we will use such phrases as "moral autonomy" or "second-order autonomy" as a shorthand, as if the subject matter or level of operation qualified the nature of the autonomy itself. These pairs of distinctions, first/second order and moral/non-moral, intersect so that there can be either moral or non-moral first-order autonomy, moral or non-moral second-order autonomy. We will discuss them together because the moral/non-moral distinction is easily made out, and because there is an influential tradition of philosophers which restricts the scope of autonomy to the moral, second-order sphere. Hence, taking up these pairs of distinctions together will enable us to assess straightforwardly this particular, pivotal view of autonomy.

A. First-Order Autonomy

First-order autonomy is autonomy exercised in the particular decisions which occupy us in the ordinary course of life: where to live, whom to marry, what vocation to pursue. And, of course, the still more concrete choices that arise within these domains, those which pertain to the details of our home, family, and work. These everyday decisions can be made more or less autonomously, depending, as we have seen, on our resources, abilities, and freedom from restrictions.

While the examples just cited are by and large non-moral, first-order autonomy can also be employed in moral matters. Deciding on whether to support a political candidate on moral grounds, to tell a lie to protect a friend, or how to discharge a filial obligation are instances of autonomy exercised in first-order, moral matters. As is fairly evident, the only difference between the moral and non-moral exercise of autonomy in first-order decisions concerns content or subject matter. The conditions which encourage or hinder autonomous decision-making in first-order moral affairs are the same as for the non-moral concerns. We can be coerced, manipulated, or unable to disobey an authoritarian parent regardless of the morality or amorality of the matter at hand.

B. Second-Order, Moral Autonomy

Some philosophers construe autonomy as essentially moral by confining its domain to second-order moral deliberations and choices. In this, they are allied with Kant. Kant viewed autonomy as moral self-legislation: the individual authoring his moral principles, obeying moral laws he has given himself. The autonomous individual does not simply conform to some conventional standard of conduct. Rather, he rationally ascertains for himself what is "willable" by any and for any rational agent. He is autonomous because not under the influence of his contingent desires or ambitions, but governed by the fruits of a dispassionate, disinterested rationality. Autonomy for Kant is the freedom to determine practical reason through a principle of reason itself, and doing so!

More recently, Gerald Dworkin and Stanley Benn have offered more detailed, less abstract interpretations of autonomy as second-order moral decision-making. What I have called first-order autonomy, Benn refers to as "autarchy," reserving "autonomy" for the ideal of critical self-reflection. The individual's beliefs, values, and principles are "his because the outcome of a still-continuing process of criticism and re-evaluation."[22] This is in contrast to the heteronomous person who is "a slave to convention, choosing by standards he has accepted quite uncritically from his milieu."[23] Benn doesn't think that autonomy requires an individual to conjure his conceptual schemes or criteria of evaluation out of thin air. Rather, autonomy requires critical appraisal of social standards, perhaps by means of canons derived from another strand of one's tradition, in the quest for coherence and cogency.

According to Benn, the autonomous individual discovers who he "really is" through reflection on critical choices, as he discovers that principles and attitudes hitherto taken to define his personality have become eroded.[24] This requires the self-awareness of second-order moral reflection lacking in the heteronomous individual. "The heteronomous man looks in his uncertainty to others for cues, or he clings to the habitual."[25] Benn suggests that the heteronomous man clings to the habitual because he is unwilling to rethink who he is or because of social pressures to conform. But other explanations exist, such as the lack of awareness bred by a mechanical identification with a particular viewpoint. Stefan Arkadyevitch, Anna Karenina's brother, is a classic example. He borrows his beliefs from a liberal newspaper, unaware that he does so, and incapable of defending why they are correct. His views change as the paper's do, imperceptibly and unselfconsciously.[26]

Dworkin elaborates on autonomy as the "second-order judgments we make concerning first-order considerations." The autonomous person can formulate an attitude towards the influences on his thinking and behavior.[27] He can then decide what sort of person to be by embracing or disowning certain of his characteristics. Dworkin refines the concept of autonomy by dividing it into two components, authenticity and independence.

1. AUTHENTICITY

"Authenticity" obtains when the individual identifies with his motivations, conceives and commits himself to be that sort of person. This hinges on the second-order choice of whether to affirm or disown such characteristics as his jealousy or loyalty, competitiveness or tactfulness. This kind of identification would seem to have both a judgmental and volitional component. It requires first determining what one's motivations and desires are, then deciding on whether to continue as the sort of person so motivated. Since Dworkin also speaks of autonomy as "critical, self-consious reflection on one's moral principles,"[28] his notion of authenticity should probably be supplemented with reference to commitment to principles as well. Thus, authenticity obtains when an individual identifies himself as a certain sort of person in light of reflection on his desires, interests, and moral principles.

Authenticity doesn't seem to depend on the extent to which the individual actually manages to live up to his identification, whether in fact he succeeds in being compassionate or competitive, generous or gregarious—whatever is consistent with his self-conception. Dworkin leaves aside the question of consistency in action with one's authentic self, except to say elsewhere that acting in accord with one's principles is integrity. However, as we saw in considering autonomy of will, someone who is incapable of acting in accord with his highest or most basic values and commitments is indeed lacking in autonomy. I suspect that Dworkin doesn't include this as an aspect of autonomy because he construes autonomy strictly in terms of second-order reflection/decision. First-order matters such as how one acts and whether those actions square with second-order decisions fall outside considerations of autonomy.

Yet this seems to miss an important aspect of autonomy, if not of authenticity per se. As John Kekes insightfully points out, we are capable of projecting a coherent pattern as an ideal way of life and then striving to realize it. "Constancy" is being true to this deliberate pattern that one projects for oneself.[29] (Authenticity, according to Kekes, is merely being true to the self one happens to have rather than the ideal self which one is committed to pursuing.) We might, however, ask why a "constant" person is more autonomous than one who isn't.

For one thing, the constant person is deliberate about his future; he has decided to become one sort of person rather than another (such as the one he presently is). We can also see the inconstant person as lacking in self-mastery the way someone who is pulled about by different desires lacks self-mastery. The difference is that the inconstant individual goes this way and that pursuing external goods. He is pulled in different directions from without, depending on the opportunities presented by the circumstances. Such a person lacks self-mastery because governed by events and circumstances rather than self-generated ideals and commitment.

This directly bears on the nature of Dworkin's understanding of authenticity itself. His conception of authenticity is too passive. The individual seems unduly circumscribed in his second-order deliberations by his present motivations and principles. Why can't he decide to become a different sort of person altogether, committed to a cluster of hitherto foreign values? Such a person can exercise a more radical control over who he will be. As Charles Taylor puts it, the individual can ask, "have I really understood what is essential to my identity? Have I truly determined what I sense to be the highest mode of life?"[30] True, he must reflect on his present nature, but it would seem that he can do much more than simply affirm or deny what he finds within. He can also be so impressed with another's life or ideals, for example, as to set about to alter his character in ways much more radical than Dworkin would have us imagine.

Authenticity is obviously essential to autonomy, but it will not be our major concern in what follows. Rather, we shall concentrate on questions of independence.

2. INDEPENDENCE

The significance of authenticity, however, raises the question: how did the individual arrive at his identification? By what process was the self-reflection on motivation and character-type carried out? If arrived at in an "independent" way, then the person is autonomous. For in addition to authenticity, autonomy requires that the choice of self be "one's own." And this requires what Dworkin considers "procedural independence."[31] He discloses what procedural independence is largely through negative inference, by adducing examples of interference or prevention. Manipulation, deception, and withholding information interfere with procedural independence. The individual is not making his own choice so much as being directed from without, by another.

Dworkin's idea is that the self-concept that the individual comes up with may be determined for him by another rather than himself. Even if the whole self-concept isn't chosen by another, at the very least certain possibilities for self-determination may be foreclosed by the other's interference. And that is enough to jeopardize the independence of the procedure by which the self-concept is arrived at.

On the other hand, education, logical thinking, and access to varied conceptions of moral life do not interfere with procedural autonomy. Presumably, because these sorts of influences are compatible with if not necessary for "rational" scrutiny of one's self. Quite naturally, Dworkin doesn't wish to exclude every sort of influence on an individual's self-reflection as interference; for example, he emphasizes the importance of context and traditions.

Stanley Benn goes a bit further in stressing the way a pluralistic society fosters autonomy. Pluralistic societies offer diversity in standards, values, and perspectives.[32] As a result, the individuals nurtured in such a society generally have access to these diverse viewpoints. Marilyn Friedman amplifies on this by pointing out how autonomy depends on an individual's ability to imagine alternatives to the standards which she already accepts. Consequently, "where alternatives can be found and do not have to be invented, there personal autonomy will be more easily fostered."[33] Access to a variety of viewpoints, values, even traditions, therefore, is a condition which facilitates autonomy. Conversely, unavailability of different perspectives impedes autonomy, as does the circumscription dictated by dependence.

3. DEPENDENCE

In analyzing failure to exercise procedural independence (henceforth, simply "independence"), we can augment the idea of interference with the now-familiar notion of dependence. In our earlier discussion of restrictions on autonomy, we saw how dependence on others can limit the individual's autonomy of judgment or volition. Here we take it up in terms of second-order decisions about who we are and what we wish to become. Dependence on another to make our decisions for us can be the result of interference, as when the other manipulatively brings about the dependency, but it need not be. The dependent person might, rather, be taking this "easy way out" from a weakness of will, or he could self-consciously choose to be the sort of individual who does what the Army, or the clergy, or a parent says. In an independent way, the individual reflects on what sort of person he wishes to be and decides to be the sort who obeys some particular authority. Such second-order dependence, therefore, can be the result of independent second-order decision-making. Hence we need to distinguish between whether an individual is presently independent and whether he exercised second-order independence in arriving at his present condition. We will pursue this distinction further in the next section of this chapter. More typically, the dependence simply "evolves" without a conscious self-reflective decision about the sort of person we wish to be. A young physician, for example, looks to her superior for "guidance" in deciding the proper path for herself: which values to identify with, what sort of person or physician to become. Such guidance could be relied upon, wittingly or not, as a substitute for the individual's own critical self-reflection. It need not be the product of manipulation or deception, but simply a habit of depending inordinately upon the advice of another. This seems to be the way procedural dependence develops in first-order choosing—the level at which it is more typical.

C. Second-Order, Non-Moral

The last combination to consider is second-order non-moral choice. Most self-reflection on one's values and principles will be either explicitly moral or ultimately related to moral values and principles. However, one could decide to be motivated in a particular way without specific regard to its morality. We can, with Harry Frankfurt, imagine someone who "wants to be motivated in what he does by the desire to concentrate on his work."[34] In a more encompassing decision, an individual could choose to be a certain sort of person or to make decisions in a certain sort of way without (immediately) engaging his moral values. The decision to be a self-sufficient "mountain man" could be made on prudential grounds. Or, an individual might decide to make all future decisions on the basis of expected pleasure and pain for herself. She might not reflect on the moral justification of her decision but simply see it as most productive of a balance of pleasure over pain without questioning either her hedonism or egoism.

Although Dworkin restricts questions of authenticity (and autonomy in general) to second-order, moral deliberations, this seems misplaced. It certainly makes sense to contrast those who critically assess their underlying non-moral habits, values, and principles with those who don't. People can easily fall into patterns of thought and action in non-moral avenues of life—the habits of pessimistic thinking or compulsively tidy housekeeping, for example. To the extent that an individual "steps back" and assesses these non-moral dimensions of self, to that extent he is authentic.[35]

Clearly, then, autonomy can be exercised in second-order non-moral matters. However, it seems reasonable to think that second-order autonomy is "incomplete" without an accompanying moral reflection to appraise critically the assumptions upon which it rests. A person who does subject his assumptions to such further self-reflection is no doubt more autonomous than one who does not. But just as surely is an individual who engages in only second-order non-moral deliberation more autonomous than one who doesn't engage in any second-order reflection at all.

D. First-Order Decisions, Re-examined

It is instructive at this point to look at Dworkin's reasons for confining autonomy to second-order moral decisions.[36] He believes that people have little or no control over the varied influences on their thinking and behavior. So it is beside the point to speak of autonomy in first-order matters. The preferences, desires, wishes, habits, and emotions that people have are pretty much beyond their control. On the other hand, "the autonomous individual is able to step back and formulate an attitude towards the factors that influence his behavior."[37] The ability to formulate such an attitude is captured by the notion of authenticity. But Dworkin's position on what we can control is either too strong or too weak to be compatible with his own understanding of autonomy. On the strong interpretation, the possiblity of autonomy (as both authenticity and independence) is called into question. On the weak interpretation which allows for the second-order autonomy Dworkin argues for, first-order autonomy must also be granted.

Let's consider first how Dworkin's position is too strong for his *own* sense of autonomy. If Dworkin's worry about determinism and our lack of control over the influences on our behavior is taken seriously, then why not extend it to: (a) the "attitude" we take towards these influences (and the possibility of authenticity); and, (b) the so-called procedural independence, which is the other facet of autonomy? Why should we think that the attitude we take towards the influences on our behavior is any more in our control than those influences themselves? Surely we may just as well have been conditioned to accept or reject our jealousy, compassion, or competitiveness: our future self in question. In addition, the whole notion of "procedural independence" becomes suspect. Our so-called independent choice of self-concept could be merely the outcome of social forces over which we have no awareness or power. It would seem to matter little whether our second-order decision-making has been "interfered" with since its contours are beyond our control in the first place.

On the other hand, if we do indeed have control over what attitude we take towards the influences on our behavior (authenticity) as well as over the manner and content of our second-order moral decisions (procedural independence), then there is no good reason to confine procedural independence to second-order decision-making. It would seem just as plausible to think that individuals can be more or less independent in their choice-making at the level of everyday, first-order matters. Dworkin has not provided a principle by which to establish that we are self-determining only at the "meta" level.

Second-Order Values and Principles

Before shifting our attention to the relationship between autonomy and other dimensions of personal life, I'd like to consider some revealing connections between autonomy and the nature of one's second-order values and principles. The content of one's basic values and principles helps determine the extent to which an individual enjoys first or second-order autonomy. That is, certain second-order principles are autonomy-regarding; they influence the exercise of autonomy, on either level, within their scope. It is thus helpful to distinguish between autonomy-affirming and authoritarian (autonomy-denying) basic principles.

Since this chapter's emphasis is more on hindrances to and inhibitions of autonomy, we'll concentrate on the impact of authoritarian basic principles and values. Once in place authoritarian principles limit first-order autonomy. The individual will more or less do what others, directly or through some text or procedure, tell him to do in a range of matters. Given a basic commitment to heed a religious or parental authority for example, first-order autonomy in deciding such matters as whom to marry or where to live would be lacking.

Reference to these basic principles and values helps capture what Gerald Dworkin calls "substantive" dependence and independence. Substantive dependence, as the term suggests, refers to the "substance" or content of what one does. It indicates that one is conforming one's behavior to the behavior of others. By adopting the purposes or goals of another, the individual is following the other's life rather than fashioning a substantively different one. As I construe it, substantive dependence (at least of the self-conscious variety) is a form or result of the procedural dependence attendant on adopting authoritarian basic principles and values. These basic principles and values stipulate *how* first-order decisions are made and what sort of life the individual is to lead: such as, in conformity with Marxist teaching, church doctrine, or parental fiat. Substantive dependence then is either built into the authoritative text/person or follows from it.[38]

But what of the second-order autonomy of the individual with authoritarian basic principles? Authoritarian principles would seem to discourage the individual from scrutiny of himself as well as those very authoritarian principles. Authorities and scripture, for example, do not speak only to first-order choices, but are also self-referring. They include within their scope the bases of their own authority, their own legitimation. As such, authoritarian basic principles are unrevisable. Their content closes off the possibility of criticism and subsequent change. In this way, these principles are self-preserving.

The upshot is that a person who subscribes (self-consciously or not) to authoritarian basic principles relinquishes second-order autonomy, or at least the commitment to it (since such renunciation is not easily made irrevocable). Once again we see the value of the notion of procedural dependence. In such situations it need not be the case that the individual is having his procedural independence interfered with. Rather, he may simply have become dependent—on the authority denoted in the basic principles.

Here we return to the restriction of first-order autonomy. By sealing themselves off from the critical self-reflection constitutive of second-order autonomy, authoritarian principles ensure continued lack of first-order autonomy. The content of our second-order principles can limit first-order autonomy directly, by prescribing procedural dependence over a particular domain, such as whom to marry, whether to bear arms, and the like. It can also limit our first-order autonomy indirectly by stipulating second-order procedural dependency. The second-order dependency on a church elder, for instance, to decide matters of marriage and vocation, deprives the individual of his first-order autonomy.

It is important to note that the content or nature of these second-order principles is somewhat independent of the manner by which they come to be held. We need to distinguish how autonomous an individual is as a consequence of his second-order values and principles from how autonomously these values and principles were acquired. It is at least possible that a person autonomously (with procedural independence) comes to hold authoritarian basic principles. Even though these principles subsequently limit his autonomy on either or both levels, the individual may have chosen them autonomously. Conversely, we can imagine someone manipulated into accepting second-order principles which affirm autonomy and require his self-reliance.

As implausible or unlikely as these combinations may be, they not only seem possible, but particular instances come to mind. Religious people may come to accept church authority only after great struggle and self-examination; the authoritarian principles they then come to hold are autonomously arrived at. On the other hand, "liberal" parents may inculcate the importance of independence in a way that itself interferes with their children's independence, through heavy-handed argument or the like. However, the result of such indoctrination may be that the child subscribes to autonomy-affirming basic principles. Thus, the nature of the basic values and principles is somewhat independent of whether autonomy is exercised in securing them.

This last example calls our attention to the alternative of autonomy-affirming priciples. Obviously, such principles don't call for the individual to subordinate his own judgment and decision-making to others. Even where he is required to abide by a decision he might (in "principle") disagree with, as with democratic principles, his own autonomy plays a role in the overall procedure. The individual makes proposals, questions, argues and finally votes, according to democratic principles. As the case of democratic commitments indicates, autonomy-affirming principles take into account the exercise of others' autonomy as well. Thus do principles of truth-telling, fairness, and rationality respect autonomy per se and not just the agent's autonomy. The importance of this universal "scope" is underscored by the fact that for these principles to be revisable and admit of indefinite scrutiny, the input of other people is pivotal. Thus, in order for the individual to hold these principles in an autonomous manner, their meaning must comprehend the autonomy of others.

When a principle or value concerning some particular matter is "autonomy-affirming," it is appropriately "informed." A commitment to education or the valuing of marriage, for example, are given specific shape when autonomy-affirming. Education and marriage mean something different when informed by fidelity to autonomy than when not. Probably the most basic and general autonomy-affirming value and principle is respect itself. The next chapter articulates a concept of moral respect and outlines the sorts of demands it makes on us.

One other connection between autonomy and our basic values ought to be mentioned. Conflict in first-order decision-making or indecision often occasions re-examination of our basic principles and values. If we think that life is sacred, for example, but find another's or our own excruciating suffering with terminal illness intolerable, we will be forced to re-examine life as an absolute value. Sometimes this conflict-induced self-reflection will result in the modification of a principle, sometimes in the actual rejection or addition of a value. Someone who holds to a certain rigorism in punishment, for example, could find himself so moved by the wrongdoer's extenuating circumstances as to introduce the concept of mercy into his system of basic values.

Where does our discussion leave us, so far? Autonomy, as independence, can be exercised in either first or second-order decisions. These decisions can be either moral or non-moral. Obstacles to autonomy may be internal or external, but lack of autonomy is not always due to obstacles or interference. Autonomy can be supplanted by dependence, which itself admits of a variety of origins. Moreover, autonomy develops and flourishes with the help of certain conditions, abilities, and resources. Some of these are external to the individual, such as economic and cultural resources. Some come from within, such as intellectual abilities. In addition, some of our basic values and principles affect how autonomously we function. It is therefore important to distinguish autonomy-denying principles from those which affirm the development and exercise of autonomy.

Autonomy is both fostered and frustrated, encouraged and restricted, by our interactions with others. The rest of the book is devoted to examining specific kinds of interactions and relationships. I will now take up the sorts of interactions and relationships dictated by moral respect. In the process I will examine the theoretical question of how and why autonomy is the basis for respect.

CHAPTER TWO

Respect and Autonomy

This chapter is concerned with moral respect; in particular, the sort of respect which is due anybody, just because he or she exists. Because it is owed anyone, regardless of accomplishment or failure, we can consider this sort of respect "unearned." It stands in constrast to earned respect, the sort due only some people, by virtue of something particularly good which they have done or are. People earn our respect because of their accomplishment, while others do not since they have done nothing especially worthwhile. While unearned respect is moral, earned respect would at least appear to be both moral and non-moral.

The term "respect" is obviously used loosely in everyday life. In what follows, I shall have to clarify, even modify that ordinary usage. This is to be expected, since the result of much moral philosophy is a sharpening and developing of common concepts. In the course of these clarifications and modifications, I will try to take ordinary usage into account and not simply bypass it in favor of a more sophisticated rendition. Before addressing unearned respect, a little bit should be said about earned respect, especially since it bears, if only indirectly, on our main topic.

Earned Moral Respect

Earned moral respect most obviously refers to the respect someone deserves in light of some moral achievement—good character or works. Thus we say that Smith is owed moral respect because his great personal sacrifice provided tremendous benefit to his community or that Jones deserves our respect because he exemplifies so many virtues. Earned moral respect can also be for the level or extent to which someone exercises her autonomy. Here there seem to be at least two levels.

On the level of daily choice, we respect people for "making their own decisions:" deciding where to live, what career to pursue, for whom to vote. We tend to respect people who rely on themselves rather than others in making these first-order decisions, especially when they require overcoming obstacles such as cultural or peer pressures. On a deeper level, someone who sets his own standards and critically evaluates his values exercises greater autonomy than one who simply conforms to the standards and values (moral or otherwise) or others. Individuals can exercise autonomy over who and what they are, reflecting on the sort of person they ought to be and then trying to realize their ideals. We earn moral respect by exercising autonomy in these second-order decisions, decisions *about* values, standards, and principles.

The degree of autonomy exercised is somewhat irrespective of its fruits—the nature of the values arrived at or the life led. Thus, one could exercise a great degree of autonomy in living a nondescript or despicable life. Conversely, one could exercise little autonomy as one merely mimicked the exemplary life of, say, an Albert Schweitzer or Mother Theresa. Yet, it would be a mistake to think that the degree of autonomy and its consequences have no bearing on one another as far as earning moral respect. It would seem for example, that *some* degree of autonomy must be exercised in order for the individual to deserve respect for a moral achievement. The lack of reflection and choice in the Mother Theresa imitator makes the virtuous conduct accidental, less truly tied to the individual than if autonomy had been exercised. The individual *could* just as easily have latched onto a thief or murderer as his "model." Perhaps we actually respect the sort of life led rather than the (imitative) person leading it in this case. Obviously, there are a number of interesting relationships between the degree of autonomy exercised and its results which cannot be explored here.

Besides earned moral respect is what may be called earned "technical" respect: the sort of respect owed people in virtue of some sort of non-moral accomplishment, such as artistic virtuosity, ground breaking scientifc theorizing, or athletic prowess. Now this earned technical respect *seems* fairly unproblematic, but I would like to suggest that at bottom it may really be earned moral respect. I propose that when we respect a person for some non-moral accomplishment, say artistic virtuosity, it is because of her effort, perserverance, discipline—the moral qualities needed to perfect her talents. The musical ability or performance is rather the object of appreciation, not respect.

This becomes more obvious in light of cases of "idiot savants" or people who are "naturals." In such cases there is no question of respecting the person; we just savor the performance and marvel at the ability. When we *say* we 'respect' someone for some technical accomplishment, then, perhaps we are loosely covering two responses: respect for the moral qualities required for the accomplishment, and appreciation for the prerequisite talent. The moral qualities which we respect may be specific virtues, such as discipline and patience, or they may involve autonomy—needed to overcome the authority of parents or the tyranny of social pressure.[1]

If this hunch is correct, then all earned respect turns out to be earned moral respect. Since unearned respect is also moral, all respect is moral. I offer this simply as a pertinent suggestion; nothing that follows turns upon it. What I shall spend the rest of the discussion on is unearned moral respect, the sort of respect owed just anyone, regardless of his achievements, moral or otherwise.[2] Two questions must then be considered: on what grounds do we owe this respect; and, what does showing respect require of us?

Autonomy Grounds Unearned Respect

On what grounds do we owe someone, anyone, this unearned moral respect (hereafter simply "respect")? Although in the Kantian tradition which locates the ground of respect in autonomy, I understand autonomy here in a broader sense. Kant viewed autonomy as moral self-legislation: the individual authoring his moral principles, obeying moral laws he has given himself. Autonomy is the positive, moral concept of freedom—freedom to determine practical reason specifically through a principle derived from reason itself.[3]

The conception of autonomy employed here, as seen in the last chapter, is broader, comprehending the abilities and dispositions which make us self-determining. It is not limited to moral choices, but rather comprises life choices in general. Autonomy clearly includes the ability to reason, make deliberate choices, and be responsible for our actions and their consequences. It is the ability and disposition to make plans and decide for oneself what to do. As R.S. Peters elaborates, "Choice. . . is too narrow a concept. It does not cover such things as the grasp of rules, the formulation and statement of intentions,. . ."[4] Peters aligns autonomy with the "assertive" point of view, which includes judgments, appraisals, and decisions embedded in stable dispositions.

There is another important sense in which the conception of autonomy invoked here departs from a strict Kantian rendition. For Kant, autonomy is an "abstract" ability in the sense that it is the same in everyone and unaffected by material ("natural") conditions. As a noumenal power, the natural accidents that differentiate people are not relevant to it and neither are the real-life circumstances in which these people find themselves.[5] On my more earthly understanding of autonomy, it can be hindered or encouraged by the individual's circumstances. All sorts of things affect the development, degree, and opportunity for the exercise of autonomy. For example, coercion typically limits autonomy (at least immediately), but access to information usually enhances it. Autonomy is a matter of degree, then, depending on the individual's abilities and situation in the world. Later we shall have a chance to see what bearing this has on the demands made by respect.

But why, it may be asked, should we think that autonomy is the basis of respect? Let's view the question from two sides.

First, from the side of the value of autonomy and then from consideration of the nature of respect.

We need to examine the value of autonomy to see why *autonomy* in particular and not something else demands respect. The value of autonomy (or anything else, for that matter) can reside in itself or in its relationship to something else. The first type of value is often referred to as "intrinsic," the second, as "extrinsic." Let's see what can be said on behalf of the idea that autonomy, or living autonomously, is intrinsically valuable.

A. The Intrinsic Value of Autonomy

I'd like to consider what may broadly be construed as an Aristotelian account of autonomy as "natural": the autonomous life as a full life, proper to human beings. Lawrence Haworth makes a good case for the notion that the tendency toward autonomy is natural, and that autonomy is a natural trait. Haworth argues, "when a trait is natural the organism whose trait it is, . . . is programmed to develop it."[6]

A natural trait *grows;* it is something the individual does and can't be made to do. Of course, conditions from the organism's surroundings are needed to initiate and develop the trait. But this still contrasts with changes that are imposed from outside the organism, like forcing right-handedness on a left-handed child or cutting someone's hair. The growth of a natural trait is also different from learned dispositions or abilities, such as dancing or computer programming. While the latter are no doubt based on natural traits, they are still distinct from them.[7] Fostering a child's natural tendency to function autonomously is more like providing for the natural development of a trait in an animal, the burrowing of a hedgehog or the running of a deer, for example.[8] Haworth's claim, then, is that human beings are naturally creatures with the tendency to formulate their own projects and decide for themselves what to do. Studies in developmental psychology and behavior, in fact, bear out the view that children seek out and delight in opportunities for independent activity.[9]

If this is right, then we still need to add that there is at least a *presumption* in favor of not interfering with and even fostering the natural. This yields an argument for the presumption of fostering the development of autonomy in people in general, and those close to us in particular. This means that an overriding reason is needed to justify interfering with or failing to develop a person's autonomy. Obviously, there may be natural tendencies, such as the tendency to be aggressive or possessive, that we ought not foster. But there are good reasons which override the presumption to nurture them. At least some of these reasons concern other natural developments, for example, the way such negative tendencies as aggression thwart the natural growth of others (as well as the individual in question).

There is another important difference between such tendencies as aggression and the tendency toward autonomy. Aggression is usually specific, like gluttony or avarice, and pertains to a limited sphere of action. An individual is aggressive at work, or with regard to certain values, or with particular people. Autonomy is more general, encompassing a way of living—more the way "social" or "rational" define a life (as Aristotle would point out). It characterizes the manner in which someone lives his life, or at least large areas of it. Even though an aggressive person may display his aggression in a range of contexts, the aggression is isolable in a way that autonomy is not. Aggression can be curbed or channelled; autonomy defines the very status of the individual.

As with Aristotle's own notion of the natural, the one being considered here has a normative side. The natural isn't simply what will come to pass if the organism is left untended, at least for the human. Rather, it is what we conceive its flourishing to be, what defines a complete life. By looking at the alternative(s) to living an autonomous life, this normative dimension stands out. Living *non*-autonomously means that all or some of the following characterize one's life: dependency; inability to think independently or evaluate options critically; weakness of will. Such a life seems less than one we would consider a fully human life. Perhaps the reason for this harkens back to Haworth's "natural tendency" approach; we find such a life one in which a distinctively human potential has been stifled. It is certainly not a life we aspire to as an ideal. The person living this life is "weak" in one or more fundamental ways. We find someone who is dependent, incapable of critical reasoning, or under the sway of her emotions and appetites incapable of the sort of functioning constitutive of a full human life.

B. The Extrinsic Value of Autonomy

If this sort of Aristotelian approach is less than adequate as an account of the intrinsic value of autonomy, surely the necessity of autonomy for other values should be decisive in establishing its value. Let's turn then to the relationship between autonomy and other good things to see its extrinsic value.

Autonomy is the basis for moral behavior and responsibility, in a word—moral agency. Without autonomy individuals cannot cogently be held responsible for their conduct or deserve praise and blame. People who are governed by external forces, are dependent on others, or who can't control their own impulses lack moral responsibility. Autonomy is also essential to moral agency in the deeper sense of self-reflection. As indicated in the previous chapter, self-consciously reflecting on one's values and choosing the life we lead define a more complete autonomy. This more complete autonomy, moreover, enhances the individual's moral agency. The more we scrutinize our values and act in light of such scrutiny, the more moral agency we exhibit.

Here it may be helpful to distinguish among different sorts of extrinsic relationships in order to clarify different sorts of extrinsic value. Autonomy is valuable for the moral life as a *constituent* of it; it makes up a large and essential core of moral being. This "constitutive" relation and value should be distinguished from other sorts of extrinsic relations and values. In particular, the relation and value of instrumentality.

When something is of instrumental value for the attainment of something else, it is a means to that end. Typically, once that end is achieved, the instrumentally good thing is no longer needed. It is dispensable. Once we've hammered the boards together we no longer need the hammer; once we've reached home we can dispense with the taxicab. Whereas, when something is constitutively valuable, it persists in that thing whose goodness it helps constitute. It is not dispensable. Instead, it has a more "intimate" and enduring relationship with the valued thing. I point this out here to emphasize the essential role of autonomy in the moral life. Autonomy is not merely a means to the attainment of moral living (the way money is a means to being generous); it is constitutive of such living. So, even if autonomy has but an extrinsic relationship to moral living, it is more than simply a means to this moral status.

Again in Aristotelian fashion, it might be worthwhile to note that functioning as a moral being is in some sense "natural" to humans. We hold that denying someone moral status always requires explanation (such as severe deficiency in rationality) or justification (such as forfeiture of said status). For us, the moral is the "natural."

One of Mill's defenses of liberty also supports the "constitutive" value of autonomy. Mill agrues that happiness consists, in part, in the fullest development of people's natural endowments.[10] It isn't just that by developing these endowments we are better positioned to do the things that will bring us happiness, though this is true. Rather, it is that *part* of being happy resides in developing and exercising our distinctive human potential: to reason, perceive, imagine, evaluate, decide, and so forth.[11]

Mill's more instrumental argument for liberty leads directly to our next consideration: the value of autonomy as the means to realizing all sorts of good things. The more autonomous we are, the more choices or options we have. Given the complexity and changeability of the world, having more options would seem better than having fewer—to realize whatever values one has, including happiness. Autonomy is also needed to discover valuable things or to come to re-evalutate what one now deems worthwhile.

As Mill argues in his defense of liberty, we can't do a very good job figuring out how others should live so as to maximize their happiness. The best alternative, then, is to let them decide for themselves how to live. The individual is (usually) in the best position to decide what living well is for him and how to pursue it. By being autonomous the individual is more likely to know herself and how to match that self with the world's opportunities. The best that we can do for others is to help them develop into autonomous people. This follows from our inability to guide others in the particulars of how they should live and the plausibility of Mill's hypothesis that the individual is usually in the best position to determine his or her own happiness.

C. Respect as Appropriate to Autonomy

The second direction from which to view the link between respect and autonomy emphasizes the *general* nature of both autonomy and respect. It deals with why autonomy requires respect, rather than some other response. Since unearned respect is not for any particular achievement, what's left is some general ability or characteristic. This is fitting because respect is not a particularized attitude or response; it is general, imposing minimal constraints on our behavior.

Respect is but one moral response among many. Autonomous beings are the object of respect; however, they may also be the object of more than respect (just as non-autonomous beings may be entitled to all sorts of non-respect considerations)[12]. Noting the array of moral responses, attitudes, and concerns *besides* (and beyond) respect discloses more clearly the reason autonomy calls for respect rather than some other attitude or treatment. Think, for example, of such responses as sympathy, gratitude, or forgiveness. These are not called for by autonomy. We don't forgive someone simply because he is autonomous; neither do we feel gratitude or sympathy for this reason. Rather, we forgive the repentant, feel gratitude for kindness, and sympathize with suffering. Some of these responses, such as sympathy, don't even require autonomous beings as their object. These are moral concerns which oblige us to do different things, if not always more, than are required by respect.[13]

Respect is different from these other moral responses and concerns. It is independent of the conditions which properly govern them. While some of these other attitudes and concerns may presuppose autonomy, the way forgiveness presupposes autonomy as a condition of responsibility, they are not directed *at* autonomy. Autonomy alone is not their ground. Autonomy by itself calls for a more general, impersonal attitude or response—respect.

To say that autonomy is the ground of respect is to say that autonomous individuals are the "proper object" of respect. This is because autonomy is embodied in people. To respond to the ground of respect is necessarily to respond to its embodiment, its "proper object." Although the actual ability to function autonomously is the basis of respect, potential or capacity for it (as in infants), may oblige respectful treatment. We will see why this is so at the conclusion of the chapter.

The ground of respect is crucial, for it determines the nature of respectful behavior or treatment. The ground is automomy, but it is necessarily connected with purposiveness: not only the *ability* people have to set goals, but the actual interests and ends that they have. This is to say that autonomy is essentially teleological. Autonomy must be concerned with some purposes or other or it could not be practical. There would be no reason to deliberate, choose, and act in a self-determining fashion, nothing to deliberate or choose *about*. While purposiveness may not be part of the ground of respect; therefore, it necessarily enters into considerations of respectful treatment. These purposes as well as the individual's ability to pursue them individualize autonomy, determining its avenues of exercise. Thus, while we don't respect a person *because* of his individuality (in unearned respect), we do respect him *in* his individuality. We take his interests, purposes, and degree of autonomy itself into account in the particular way we treat him. To that treatment, then, we now turn.

Autonomy as the Object of Respect

Although respect is no doubt an attitude or disposition, I am concerned here with what it obliges us to do rather than with its psychological configuration. For someone lacking the attitude or disposition of respect, it still makes sense to say that she is nevertheless obliged to show it. What does showing respect amount to?

Autonomy, embodied in individual people, is the object of respect. Showing respect requires acting in ways which take the individuals autonomy into account. As B. J. Diggs puts it, "treating each person in ways consistent with the person's developing and freely exercising his capacity as a rational being to govern himself."[14] But this clearly needs specifying. Recall that a person's purposes and desires individuate his autonomy. They give it flesh in the real world. Are we then obliged out of respect to further the individual's ends, and if so, which ones and how much?

What argues in favor of our obligation to further people's ends is that pursuit of our ends and the satisfaction of our desires gives expression to our autonomy. If respect is at root regard for autonomy, then perhaps respect demands that we support its varied manifestations. But this seems too much to require simply of respect. Autonomy may be needed for all sorts of enterprises, all sorts of possible behavior its expression. To be required out of respect to further the expression of autonomy *simpliciter* seems too broad. This is required, rather, by general obligations of beneficence, duties arising out of special relationships (such as result from promises and role assumptions), and the call of the supererogatory. If helping just anyone in his pursuit of just anything were demanded of respect, there wouldn't be much left over to be required by the many non-respect obligation-imposing relationships and considerations.

This doesn't mean that respect has nothing to say about the pursuit of ends and the satisfaction of desires. Because they are indeed the expression of people's autonomy, showing respect requires that they not be interfered with. This is the "negative" force of respect, prohibiting certain kinds of interference and intrusions. When we refrain from such interference we show regard for autonomy by leaving people to work out their life plans. We allow them to choose and act for themselves. This might help explain the "demands of decency"—minor benefits we seem somehow obliged to confer on strangers. Giving a helping hand to a stuck motorist or a shopper struggling with packages seems obligatory, but only when the cost to us is negligible. Doesn't respect oblige us to provide assistance by doing little, low-cost favors? If so, it may be because *not* providing this low-cost help *practically* amounts to hindering the individual's exercise of autonomy.

Respect, then, doesn't require that we further all the expressions of others' autonomy. It does demand that we not interfere with them, without good reason. Rather, when respect makes positive demands on us, that we do something, it speaks directly to *autonomy*. Thus, respect requires that we help people secure what's needed to develop and exercise autonomy: the capacities constitutive of self-governance. This enables *them* to make decisions effectively in the pursuit of their own ends. We can show respect both collectively and as individuals. Providing for the health, protection, and education of its members are ways that society collectively shows them respect. The question of which institutions, laws, and forms of social organization are essential to treating a group of people with respect is obviously important. In what follows, however, I shall focus instead on what it is to show respect as individuals to individuals, moreover, to individuals we know—acquaintances, friends, relatives—rather than strangers.

Respect as Acceptance

Let's begin with a popular conviction that expresses something basic to showing respect: the belief that we should "accept people for what they are." This common view usually suggests something akin to absolute tolerance—unquestioning, uncritical embracing of the individual exactly as he or she is. It seems to preclude any sort of criticism, viewing criticism as a kind of rejection of who the individual is. But this is an indulgent understanding of acceptance, one which seems to say in the face of criticism: "Well, that's just the way he is," or "I am." This understanding of acceptance is actually closer to resignation than a true display of respect, since criticism may in fact be *required* by acceptance.

The truth contained within this popular view is captured in George Nakhnikian's "realistic" approach to acceptance: "To accept him as he is, not as we imagine him to be or as we would wish him to be . . . being disposed not to sit in magisterial judgment over him."[15] When the popular view eschews criticism, it is due to an identification of criticism with what Nakhnikian calls "magisterial judgment": belittling, ridiculing, condemning, spurning. It is this denigrating behavior that acceptance opposes.

But what of someone who truly is terrible—a Hitler or Charles Manson? Even here we can distinguish reasoned moral judgment and punishment from denigrating behavior. To judge in a court of law and subsequently either punish or "treat" is a form of respectful behavior. To punish is to acknowledge the individual's autonomy in wrongdoing, and to provide treatment is to attempt to restore the individual to autonomy. Avoiding denigrating behavior is the negative or passive side of acceptance. But acceptance also makes more positive, active demands upon us, including criticizing the individual in question.

Accepting someone for what he is now includes seeing his potential and having *realistic* expectations for his future growth or improvement. Potential for the acquisition and development of various capacities and abilities partly defines who the individual is. What is germane to respect is the potential upon which autonomous functioning turns: potential for reasoning, deliberating, evaluating, choosing. Failure to question or criticize may overlook features of the person which limit his autonomy. Respect implies a realistic regard for the individual. Realistic regard necessarily includes assessing potential for autonomy and facilitating its realization. Since criticism may be required to facilitate such growth, criticism may be positively required by the demands of respect (and not merely compatible with them).

Because what a person is also includes his beliefs, values, and purposes, acceptance requires taking them into account. Some sort of positive action may be required of us because these ingredients of personhood are so intimately tied to autonomy. The specific ways people exercise their autonomy turn upon the various configurations of these beliefs, values, and purposes. Bernard Williams[16] claims that each individual sees himself and the world from his own point of view. Respect, then, requires "identifying the individual in his own terms." This is to view the person in a way in which he is equal to all of us, as a "subject."

What exactly is involved in this "identification?" It requires sensitivity to the individual's particular ends and purposes, on the one hand, and his viewpoints and values, on the other. Let's examine them in turn. Identifying another in his own terms requires taking his point of view with regard to his own ends and interests. This entails avoiding the paternalistic impulse to impose our concept of his ends or interests. We can fail to acknowledge the other's ends out of the best of motives, that is not the point. Rather, neglecting to take the other's purposes seriously is a failure of respect. As Onora O'Neill puts it, "This failure of respect entails failure to share those ends,. . . they are either invisible or else not the other's ends but rather the ends to be sought for the other."[17]

This is especially important when what we do affects someone else. When we are considering an action which will affect another, respect requires that we make a rational assessment from that person's viewpoint. Determining what is reasonable from another's point of view is not the same as figuring "what would be reasonable to oneself if one were in the other's position in certain limited respects?"[18]

This idea has direct implications for discourse. For one, it obliges us to discuss our conduct with others to discover their viewpoint and how they see our behavior. For another, it requires "being prepared to give reasons for our actions whenever the interests of others are materially affected,"[19] or when we interfere with the autonomy of others. It is not enough to assess how the other judges his interests and the impact of our behavior on them. Treating another with respect sometimes dictates that we explain ourselves; we sometimes "owe an explanation." This shows respect both for the particular interests affected as well as for the other's more general capacity to understand reasons and grant their force.

This last issue brings us to the way in which identifying another in his own terms requires a proper regard for his values, beliefs, and perspectives. To what does such identification commit us? If it means to judge him as he judges himself, then we would have to grant his value judgments as justified. This is obviously too strong. As Robert Arrington points out, we would have to identify *with* him and, "if such identification were a necessary condition of respect, then we could not respect a person with whom we are in moral disagreement."[20] And this would be ironic indeed, since it is often just those with whom we disagree that we need to show respect for. Conversely, as Arrington puts it, "in a world of common conviction and common sentiment there would be little need for respect."[21]

On the other hand, showing respect would seem to require more than mere acknowledgment of another's evaluations and beliefs. While concurrence is clearly too strong a requirement, acknowledgment seems too weak. Proposing a middle ground between these two, Arrington suggests that we view the other as self-justified, as one who thinks of himself as right but is also fallible. Because we, too, are fallible, "there is no way in which we can say *absolutely* that he is not in fact justified;" therefore, his perspective is a "proper subject for continuing debate."[22] Because we cannot be *certain* of our own, antagonistic convictions, argues Arrington, we are obliged to continue (indefinitely?) to argue or debate.

I agree with Arrington that regardless of whether we approve or disapprove of them, we must treat the other's views and evaluations as interpretations of practical reality which require dialogue, debate, and persuasion. But, because Arrington requires *certitude* of our own view as justification for rejecting another's, he seems to demand of us "endless dialogue." His condition for believing oneself justified and the other's position untenable is so strong as to seem to demand infinite indulgence rather than respect. On the contrary, we *can* come to a point of justified rejection. For instance, when the other's views are inconsistent or filled with bad arguments and good faith attempts to explain their failings meet with obtuse resistance or refusal to respect our *own* perspective.

Although showing respect requires more than merely acknowledging another's perspective, it does not require interminable dialogue or infinitely suspended belief about someone's viewpoint. Sometimes, at some point, we *are* justified in laying the dialogue to rest, and moving onto another activity—especially when the other refuses to be consistent, admit error, or take *our* views seriously. We may quite reasonably, though without certitude that we are absolutely right, move onto another activity. In going about other business we are not failing to show respect to our interlocutor. Perhaps this amounts to showing oneself respect: paying proper regard to our own autonomy and interests and not wasting time in futile discussion. We owe it to ourselves to demand a certain level of reasonability from those with whom we spend our time.

Acceptance, then, requires neither uncritical tolerance of what another person is, nor unending critical dialogue with another's perspective on himself and the world. The realism which prompts our efforts to help someone develop his autonomy also counsels us to give up trying to change another's perspective when such change itself seems to be an unrealistic expectation.

Dependency

Respect requires that we try to promote the autonomy of others. In our more enduring relationships, however, we sometimes neglect people's autonomy (and fail to show them respect) just because we are trying to do *more* than simply show respect. Trying to show love or fulfill more demanding obligations (of friendship or family, for example), ironically can lead to failing to treat others with respect. Most obvious are instances of overt interfering with another's autonomy: coercion, manipulation, or shielding. But there is a less obvious danger to the autonomy of those we care about.

Focusing on another's goals and what he wants from us, we may subvert his autonomy by breeding its opposite—dependency. Nakhnikian defines dependency as "not using your own powers for affecting your own constructive growth but instead hoping, expecting, demanding that someone else do the job for you."[23] After offering this insight, however, Nakhnikian is too restrictive in his interpretation of what dependency means. He sees dependency as always irrational, "a dependent person hopes, expects, demands, to get, and, hence, he believes he can get, what is not humanly possible for him to get."[24] Why? Because he wants or demands from others what only he can do for himself.

While this is clearly part of what dependency is all about, perhaps a large part, surely one can demand of others what, in fact, they can but should not supply. And this is also part of being dependent. An individual can demand benefits from others which they can provide him with but which he ought to provide for himself, such as evaluating his options, arranging the details of his life, or excusing his behavior to others.

So, while Nakhnikian's view of dependency is correct in general, he overstates the case when he says that it is always irrational. Sometimes it is demanding of others what they cannot give or do for the individual, as when a son demands that a father make him a "success." And then it is irrational. But sometimes it is demanding what others can but should not do—the son demanding an executive position in his fathers's company. In both cases, the dependent behavior supplants autonomous action. In both sorts of cases it is detrimental to the individual because autonomy is being stunted.

Nakhnikian also overlooks the possibility that the impetus for the dependency may come from the "independent" individual, such as an authoritarian parent, rather than the dependent person himself. When we make another dependent on us, we fail to treat him with respect. We discourage the development and exercise of his autonomy by doing for him what he should be doing for himself.

At the same time, however, the dependent person fails to treat us with respect. When irrational, as Nakhnikian would have it, the dependent person is making unrealistic demands on us by expecting us to do things for him which we simply cannot do. Because he has an unrealistic view of us, the dependent person does not truly "accept" and, therefore, respect us for what we really are. On the other hand, when the dependency is rational, and we could satisfy the dependent's demands, it nevertheless encroaches on our autonomy. It saddles us with another's life, inevitably to the neglect of our own. Just as our autonomy itself is now bounded by the dependent person's needs, so are our purposes and interests disregarded by him.

Noticing these two sides of how dependency conflicts with respect reveals the dialectic between self and other. We are equally disrespectful when either being dependent on others or fostering dependency in others. In each case, moreover, we fail to show proper respect for ourselves. When encouraging dependency in another, we invite in them lack of acceptance of who *we* really are and the subsequent controlling behavior which circumscribes our autonomy. When *we* are dependent, on the other hand, we are forfeiting or trying to forfeit the opportunity to develop our autonomy the way it ought to be developed.

Unworthiness of Respect

Unearned respect is owed anyone, just in virtue of his or her autonomy. It might be wondered, though, whether there are nevertheless some kinds of people who are not worthy of respect, toward whom we are not obliged to show respect. Thomas Hill, for example, proffers, but does not endorse, the following suggestive case:

> There comes a time when we have sufficient evidence that a person is not ever going to *be* rational, moral, excellent, or autonomous even if he still has a capacity, in some sense, for being so. As a person approaches death with an atrocious record so far, the chances of his realizing his diminishing capacities become increasingly slim.[25]

As Hill describes him, the incorrigible or "moral degenerate" spans two related cases: the autonomous person with little chance of excellence, and someone whose capacities for autonomy are not likely to be realized in autonomous functioning. In the first case, insofar as the individual still possesses the abilities which comprise autonomy, he commands our respect. Autonomy need not be exercised in a morally salutary way. In the second case, however, if we really do have "sufficient evidence" that he cannot "realize his diminishing capacities" for *autonomy* (rather than its moral exercise), then the moral degenerate no longer compels our respect. A being which has lost the ability to function autonomously cannot command our respect since autonomy is the ground of respect. Care and consideration, of course, might still be required of us.

The issue of what would count as sufficient evidence that an individual would never be autonomous is a difficult epistemological question. Short of such clear-cut cases as brain damage, belief that someone who was once autonomous will never be again might be quite difficult to justify. Where it cannot be justified, and we have reason to believe that the individual's ability to function autonomously can be regained, then respect requires such rehabilitative efforts. The defense of this position is to be found in parallel considerations of children, to which I shall shortly turn.

Arrington also offers several candidates for those unworthy of respect. "There are many people who are indeed not worthy of respect,... Why should we *respect* an infant or very small child, a derelict, or an unthinking vegetable of a man?"[26] The cases of the small child and derelict are significantly different from the unthinking vegetable—let us say, someone in an irreversible coma. Arrington is correct in claiming that the latter is not worthy of respect. The comatose person is not presently autonomous and, by hypothesis, has lost the capacity for autonomy. But the young child and the derelict are a different story; autonomy is a possibility for them in a way that it is not for the comatose man.

Since the derelict is essentially the same as Hill's moral degenerate, the same observations apply to his case. If the derelict still has the abilities constitutive of autonomy, he cannot be written off, at least from the standpoint of respect. However, Arrington is right in claiming that the young child is not (presently) worthy of respect. We might actually do better to say that she is not a "suitable object" of respect, "unworthiness" more aptly applied to the matter of "earned" respect. But this is still too quick. The case is more complex, demanding a more detailed account of the requirements of respect. Because the child has the potential to become autonomous, to realize the capacities constitutive of self-determination, we are obliged to nurture them.

The major difference between the young child and the derelict is that the former's capacity for autonomy has not yet been realized. The typical derelict cannot function autonomously because, although his capacities for self-determination have been realized, his ability to function autonomously is presently obstructed or interfered with (usually by antagonistic habits or a debilitating condition). We are not required to respect the child because she does not presently have the ability to function autonomously, however, considerations of respect require that we help the child become an object of respect. To the extent that the derelict/degenerate has only the capacity, and not the actual ability to function autonomously, the same would apply to him. Helping the child become autonomous, moreover, will require respectful behavior, such as trusting the child, soliciting expressions of preference, providing contexts of choice. In fact, sometimes by granting a child more responsibility than he has quite demonstrated competence over, we do more to encourage autonomy.[27] And, as the child gradually becomes more autonomous, respect is demanded of us because the child is in fact becoming worthy of respect.

This last remark suggests that since autonomy is a matter of degree, so is respect. This is a bit misleading. Rather, there is a (vague) minimal level of autonomy requisite for being treated with respect. Then, depending on level of or potential for autonomy, showing respect will involve a range of responses. Included among such responses are those which grant the individual a certain amount of responsibility for his own life. This is not a matter of degree of respect so much as a matter of the way showing respect requires taking into account people's level of autonomy. In the case of children, and probably derelicts as well, we accord responsibility for their own affairs on the basis of both their present ability for self-governance and potential for its development. Children present us with but one example, albeit a crucial one, of how respect requires dealing with the particularities of an individual's autonomy.[28]

To this line of reasoning, it may be objected: why are we obliged to foster a child's autonomy? Why should a being's potential for autonomy impose an obligation upon us to help him or her realize it? My answer is that respect obliges us to help develop autonomous people because autonomy is the basis of moral agency.[29]

As indicated in the second section, autonomy is the basis for moral behavior and responsibility. It is necessary for an individual to be a moral being. Now, if status as a moral being is itself morally good (if only as a condition for any moral attribute), then there is a presumptive reason for helping to realize an individual's potential for it. It seems oddly difficult to know where to begin arguing for the moral goodness of the existence of moral agency, it's that basic. But perhaps we can get at it by noticing what happens when the potential for autonomy is either thwarted or neglected.

Failing to help develop a child's autonomy is like killing by omission, through inactivity if not outright obstruction. Only in the case before us it is omitting to bring a moral being into the world. All sorts of arguments can be mustered against the view that we are obliged to bring into existence every potential person. These are arguments against the wrongness of abortion or birth control: there may be plenty of people already in the world or this family; these potential people may not have very good prospects; other good things might be prevented by bringing these potential people into the world.[30] But these arguments will not hold against the view that we are obliged to develop the autonomy of an existing being. For here, where the being already exists, the question is what mode of existence it shall and should have.

As indicated earlier, the alternative to an autonomous individual (assuming that we are going to let the child live) is a dependent, slavish being. It would seem to be morally better to have an autonomous individual, capable of moral life, than a dependent one, quiet apart from the social costs of such dependency. At the very least, the presumption appears to be so. Therefore, there is at least a moral presumption against denying a child entrance into the moral realm, the "Kingdom of Ends."

The case of the child, then, is not really so different from that of a normal adult. Both require that we be concerned with the individual's autonomy and act appropriately. Like children, adults also are imperfectly autonomous. Respect requires that we help them develop their autonomy in addition to not interfering with their exercise of it. This includes "realistic" acceptance of who they are, what they believe, and what they can become. It also involves avoiding the sort of dependence, in ourselves and others, which habituates the individual away from self-governance.

CHAPTER THREE

Lying and Loss of Autonomy

Lying is a particular form of disrespect. Its pervasiveness and familiarity make it a plausible paradigm for deepening our understanding of respect — self-respect as well as respect for others. At the same time, lying is worth studying in its own right. The primary goal of this chapter, therefore, is to clarify what is wrong with lying. This we will do by focusing on autonomy and its loss. What's more, we can get clear on what is always wrong with lying, regardless of the specifics of the lie's content and circumstances. These specifics will be relevant to assessing the morality of the particular lie, of course, but even their bearing on the morality of the particular lie will be revealed by attention to how the lie impairs or threatens to impair autonomy. In our analysis we will see how lying restricts not only the deceived's autonomy, but the liar's as well. In fact, lying more deeply and profoundly jeopardizes the liar's autonomy.

What our focus on loss of autonomy will provide is an analysis of the "negative weight"[1] inherent in all lies — their common disvalue. Without presuming to be exhaustive, the view offered here holds that there are at least two inherent negative components of all lies; further, each of these inherent disvalues disposes the liar toward a particular, contingent harm. This account should also help clarify why some lies are worse than others, why some are excusable and others justifiable.

The first inherent disvalue found in lying is the immediate restriction of the deceived's autonomy. This, subsequently,

61

inclines the liar in the direction of disrespect for people. The second inherent disvalue is the self-opposition or internal conflict involved in speaking what one disbelieves. By itself, this self-opposition limits the liar's autonomy. In addition, it contingently threatens the integration of the liar's beliefs and his self-knowledge, thereby jeopardizing his autonomy still further. In both cases, the harm contingently risked pertains to the liar. The inherent disvalue is a "force for" the evil, disposing or inclining the liar in this harmful direction. This is the sense in which the inherent disvalues contain further "risks" for the liar; they put his character and belief structure at risk. While the realization of these dangers is contingent, dependent upon variables in the liar's and deceived's lives, the inherent disvalues are not. The way the disvalues are "necessary to" or "embedded" in all lying depends upon language and human psychology and will be explained in the course of the discussion. Before proceeding to it, some preliminary clarification about lying itself is called for.

Lying and Deception

It should be noted first that lying is a species of linguistic deception. Thus, non-linguistic and non-lying linguistic deception are distinct from lying. It is not obvious what follows from differentiating lying from these other sorts of deception; however, the discussion of disrespect (in the third section) raises some germane considerations. The motivation for drawing out the significance of this distinction is simply the fact that we seem to single lying out for special opprobrium.

What exactly is a lie? A person lies when he asserts something to another which he believes to be false with the intention of getting the other to believe it to be true. More precise definitions can be honed,[2] but this should capture the common sense of the concept while allowing for the following sort of important fine point. A person can assert a true statement and still be lying. In such a case, of course, he simply could not believe that it is true.

The following account, however, applies primarily to "successful" lies: statements which are indeed false and believed true by the deceived. This may seem unduly restrictive, so that whatever is established appears too limited in scope, not bearing on all lies. I don't think that this is so because the inherent negative weight of successful lies is the basis for our disapproval of lies in general. "Unsuccessful" lies (statements which are either indeed true, or false statements not believed by the would-be dupe) are derivatively discredited and suspect by being failed attempts at successful lies.[3] In a similar way do we demand justification for failed attempts to do bodily harm to another.

That lying can and often does have a wide range of harmful effects either in particular actions or as widespread practice is obvious. Because Smith is lied to, for example, he fails to do what is needed for him to secure this or that good thing. Or, again, because lying is rampant in this sector of society, great inefficiency is produced as people must check information and so forth. Such harmful consequences may or may not be produced by any particular lie or practice of lying. But the evaluation of any lie must include the "weight" of the two inherent disvalues and the respective harms they dispose us to. To justify a lie, its contingent good consequences must overshadow not only contingent bad consequences, but the inherent losses of autonomy and the dangers to which they expose the liar.

Restriction of Autonomy

All (successful) lies immediately restrict the deceived's autonomy. First of all, lies interfere with the deceived's autonomy of judgment by generating false beliefs. The dupe thinks of people and the world wrongly and then reasons incorrectly from these mistaken views. Rarely, however, is this restriction of thought confined to the realm of beliefs and inferences. Consonant with the liar's typical motive for lying is the impact false beliefs and misled reasoning have on the deceived's conduct.

He thinks mistakenly about possible courses of action which limits his choices and thereby his autonomy of action.

Believing true what is false or vice versa, the deceived's perspective on the world and his possible futures in it are distorted. As a result, his choices of action concerning the future are circumscribed. By limiting the horizon or content of his practical reasoning, the lie restricts the choosing and subsequent acting of the deceived. He reasons within a more or less false view of the world; misinformed, his practical conclusions and the actions they motivate are misdirected.

The lie misdirects the deceived's reasoning about future conduct in two complementary ways. It may suggest choices that are not available or eliminate from consideration live options. Both the illusion and elimination of choice limit the deceived's autonomy. The first makes his reasoning practically fruitless, thereby retarding or postponing the deliberations necessary to the exercise of autonomy of action. The latter excludes options from the scope of his volition; they are "shielded" from his view. In this respect, lying establishes, "conditions of unfreedom . . . [which] restrict choice by making alternatives unavailable or ineligible."[4]

Both the illusion and elimination of choice have the net effect of deflecting the dupe's reasoning. Unwarranted inferences are drawn; barren plans of action laid; irrelevant courses of inquiry opened. The lie not only determines what the deceived thinks about, but it skews how she thinks of things: for instance, whether she sees something as a threat or a boon. Misinformed and misdirected, the deceived's practical reasoning and thereby her autonomy are restricted.

In lying, the dupe's thinking is channelled through a distorted view of the world, as lying always aims to misrepresent the way things really are. But the more we see things the way they really are, the more autonomous our choices and subsequent actions. In offering a criterion for freedom as autonomy, Benn and Weinstein speak to the issue of one individual controlling the thinking of another. Though not specifically about lying, what they say is clearly germane to it: "it [criticism, choice, eventually freedom] . . . requires that B's sources of information shall not be controlled by A, for then B's view of reality is what A chooses to make it."[5]

It is important to underscore the significance of the deceived's reasoning and the liar's motivation in all this. Lying presupposes that the deceived has enough reason and memory to be affected by what people tell him, whether true or false. Attempting to get another to believe a false proposition true requires that that person have the capacity to understand, believe, and so forth: in short, that he possess autonomy of judgment. As for the liar, his speech is purposeful — aiming at an end beyond mere deception or constraint of autonomy (this will be developed shortly). The deceived's rational competency together with the liar's purposefulness explain the sense in which restricting reason, and thereby autonomy of both judgment and action, is "inherent" in or necessary to lies. Lies being what they are, the restriction is "practically" necessary — necessarily part of the practice. Lies being purposeful endeavors at getting someone capable of reasoning to hold a false belief, restricting that person's reasoning is simply how lies "work." And since restricting reasoning necessarily restricts overall autonomy, restriction of autonomy is inherent in lying.

In all cases of lying, the liar[6] is trying to channel the thinking and subsequent choosing of the other by his utterance, though this is rarely the only thing he is trying to accomplish. The restriction is usually thought to serve some further purpose. As Arnold Isenberg points out, "it is impossible to understand why, without ulterior purpose, anyone should wish another to believe a proposition, P, when he himself thinks that P is false."[7] It is a rare liar who seeks siimply to deceive. But regardless of ulterior or ultimate purpose, the lie always immediately limits the particular deliberations and choosing of the deceived. "Immediately" is important here, since it is possible to enhance the other's autonomy of judgment or action in the long run by lying. Similarly, lying may benefit the deceived in other ways as well, such as prompting him to action which yields some material benefit. These and considerations like them are what enable us to excuse or justify some lies.[8]

Even excused or justified lies, however, immediately restrict the deceived's autonomy by circumscribing the exercise of her reason. The general ability to reason is not usually impaired, rather its particular exercise is limited. The ability to reason might be impaired in an extreme sort of case, for example, a lie about the reasoning process itself. Thus, a seemingly far-fetched lie about the harmfulness of inductive reasoning (in deference, perhaps, to divination) would likely undermine the dupe's reasoning capacity itself, and consequently reduce her autonomy of judgment (and then action).

What enables us to excuse or justify a lie are its "material conditions": the content of the lie and the situation in which it occurs. These material conditions provide a basis for excusing and justifying lies because of the way they bear on how the lie restricts the deceived's autonomy. Either the content or situation in which the lie is offered are so related to his loss of autonomy that we excuse or justify the lie. Let us consider the paradigm cases of the excused "white" lie and the justified "defensive" lie. These should reveal the centrality of autonomy in the relationship between liar and deceived.

The reason we are usually so quick to forgive or excuse white lies[9] is that as a group they usually do not restrict the deceived's autonomy very much. Because of their content, typical situation, or both, lies considered "white" tend to be innocuous, not limiting the deceived's autonomy seriously or for long. One reason for this is somewhat trivial; the deceived is familiar with the social convention (standard responses to questions such as, "do you like my new tie?") and so does not take the speech as straightforward assertion. On the analysis offered by Chisholm and Feehan, because of the implicit conventions governing linguistic practice, such an assertion might not even count as a lie.

More important is the fact that we categorize a lie as "white" precisely because it does not limit autonomy very much — not just any good, such as the securing of pleasure or the like, but autonomy. The dupe's reasonong and subsequent choices are not seriously limited by the white lie. Conversely, knowing the truth in that situation or about that subject (material conditions) simply would not immediately enhance his autonomy. It seems similar to borrowing a friend's possession without his permission; borrowing his pencil typically limits his choices less than borrowing his car does. But perhaps more refinement is needed.

Perhaps we really ought to distinguish between non-white lies which just do not happen to limit the deceived's autonomy much and white lies which could, through unforseen and untoward events, restrict his autonomy quite a bit. The difference is a matter of probabilities, probabilities determined by the material conditions of content and situation. The probabilities are that a white lie will not have a serious impact on the deceived's autonomy. Pebbles have less capacity for serious harm than guns even though in a particular instance the former may in fact do more damage. So, a lie is properly classified as "white" because its impact on autonomy is expected to be minimal due to its content or situation.

White lies, as a class, tend to be about matters that are not very serious or to be so situated as not to speak seriously to important matters. The restriction of autonomy should vary proportionately with the seriousness of the lie's content or situation. By focusing on autonomy, we are able to see clearly one way the material conditions of lies provide for variation in their severity. This is necessary in order to account for excusing lies. However, one more aspect needs mention.

When excusing a lie we actually excuse the liar; her state or circumstance mitigates the blame. We excuse the "white liar," therefore, for lack of imagination or linguistic facility in being kind, generous, or simply evasive. White lies might not be needed if we could express ourselves more gracefully on the spur of the moment. Or, if we had enough foresight to plan more imaginatively, for example, a surprise party. Combined with the mildness of the lie's content or situation, we excuse the white liar for common human deficiencies. Yet what of the case when we justify a lie under serious material conditions?

Consider, as a paradigm of justified lying, the "defensive" lie: a lie which aims to defend our own or another's autonomy. The material conditions of a lie may justify it because we are sometimes justified in restricting another's autonomy, in particular, when an individual tries to constrain our autonomy as in the use or threatened use of force. When this occurs, practices that are otherwise questionable come to be candidates for morally permissible response. The usual regard we ought to have for another's autonomy is altered, perhaps enough and in such ways to permit (or even require) lying.

The limitation or attempted limitation of our autonomy changes the moral boundaries which usually confine lying precisely because lying itself is anti-autonomy. The content of the lie may provide an appropriate response to a coercive situation. The unjustified restraint of our autonomy may "free" us to lie even as it may justify the use of force, intimidation, or otherwise prohibited behavior. This is not to suggest that we are thereby freed of our moral responsibility, only that we may be freed of the moral constraints that usually obtain. The restriction of another's autonomy through lying may in fact be justified because of his threat to our autonomy. It cannot, of course, be said a priori whether or in what degree the moral boundaries shift, but simply that threat of or actual limitation of autonomy is always a relevant consideration in assessing the permissibility (or even obligatoriness) of lying.[10] The invasion of autonomy inherent in lying may be morally defendable, then, as a response to such an invasion by another.[11]

This account clarifies cases of white and defensive lies. Excusing the former and justifying the latter are thoroughly understood only when we appreciate the restriction of autonomy inherent in lies. Our understanding of excuses for some lies and justifications of others is broadened, moreover, by considering how the lie's restriction of another's autonomy poses a contingent threat to the liar's character.

Disrespect

The first inherent disvalue, restriction of the deceived's autonomy, disposes the liar to the contingent harm of disrespect. How does it do this? By limiting the deceived's autonomy, lying does not respect it. In addition, lying immediately alters the relationship between the liar and the deceived. The liar's autonomy increases vis-à-vis the deceived's with regard to the subject matter of the lie. Lying enhances the liar's positon relative to the deceived by limiting the latter's options (even though, in the long run, the liar's options and his reasoning about them may well be more limited than the deceived's, discussed in the last section).

Relative advantage is itself usually in need of justification regardless of who or what is causally responsible. Imagine, for instance, a teacher giving only one student suggestions on what to study for an examination. But the fact that one of the two parties herself brings about the alteration in relative autonomy is morally germane. It is one thing to receive advantage which may not be deserved in an unwitting or otherwise innocent way (the fortunate student above); it is another to initiate it. Responsibility for the change in the relationship endangers the liar's character. Specifically, altering the balance of autonomy by lying disposes the liar toward the general habit of disrespect.

Two things need clarification here: the sense in which both inherent disvalues "dispose" the liar toward a harmful condition; and the nature of the habit, disrespect, which we are presently looking at. Each inherent disvalue moves the liar in a harmful direction. Here we are concerned with the way in which restricting the deceived's autonomy disposes the liar toward disrespect (later we will discuss the the way self-opposition tends to inhibit belief integration and self-knowledge).

But the relationship between the inherent disvalue and the contingent harm is the same in each pair. The inherent disvalue disposes the liar to harm in the same way improper rest disposes us to mental error or irascibility. The harm is more than "accidentally" produced by the inherent disvalue, but does not necessarily follow from it. The inherent disvalue is always a force in the direction of the respective harm. Human nature being what it is, the fact that lying restricts autonomy moves the liar in a definite direction, even though he may not arrive at the destination.

This notion of contributing cause or disposing factor is exemplified daily. Treating a child with suspicion, for example, tends to generate in him furtive, duplicitous behavior. Giving reasons for our actions disposes others toward reasonableness in a way that arbitrary use of superior force does not. While this is hardly a complete account of either habit or personality development (more on the latter in the next chapter), it should clarify the sort of claim made when we say that lying endangers the liar's character or personality by means of its inherent disvalues. How does the first disvalue, restriction of the deceived's autonomy, actually promote the particular habit of disrespect? And what sort of habit is it?

This sort of habit is a character defect or vice. The relationship established through the lie, altered autonomy with regard to the subject at hand, always invites in us the general disposition to place ourselves above others in either thought or action. The deceived is immediately less autonomous relative to us because of our action. The propensity toward this sort of relationship involves regarding the other as less worthy or capable of exercising autonomy than ourselves. We are thereby encouraged by the lie to see ourselves as superior to others. This involves loss of proper perspective on ourselves as we esteem ourselves too highly, becoming arrogant. For lying is to arrogate to oneself the truth about the matter at hand as well as the truth about oneself, what we, the liar, really believe. Such loss of perspective and denigration of others is a character failing.

"Character" refers to sets of habits and dispositions. Of special moral significance are those of interpersonal prominence such as courage or honesty rather than technical kinds such as those making up driving or musical competency. In discussing the implications of lying for the liar's character we are considering one kind of contingent consequence. But it is not obviously of the utilitarian stripe, not a matter of calculating satisfactions or other transitively ordered mental states. Character is not a momentary plus or minus to be weighed against other moments of positive or negative interest. Rather, considerations of character illuminate what we are as people; they penetrate to the level of identity. We might say that they bridge the ontological and moral realms by suggesting what way of being is itself good.

Even as the liar shows disrespect for the deceived, so does he treat himself disrespectfully. The liar does not respect in deed what he believes. As I shall argue in the next two sections, what we believe partially constitutes who we are. By lying, therefore, the liar ultimately does not respect who he is. Clearly, the more serious and fundamental the beliefs gainsaid in speech, the greater the disrespect the liar shows for himself. This is because the more serious and fundamental the beliefs, the more they help define the self.

It is interesting to notice how this claim of contingent danger to the liar's character bears on the "white" lie excuse and the "defensive" lie justification. White lies arise out of concern for the other's welfare. We are trying to avoid embarrassing someone or are trying to bring some pleasure into his or her life. The impetus toward disrespect is therefore mitigated by our concern for the other's well-being (though it is possible to have little respect for those we try to help). More importantly, the tendency toward disrespect is dampened by the fact that there is little gain in autonomy vis-à-vis the deceived as a result of white lies. Because white lies typically do not involve serious restriction of the dupe's autonomy, therefore, they do not move us greatly toward disrespect.

Neither are we in danger of becoming disrespectful as a result of lying in defense of our autonomy. When justified, someone else either already has or is trying to constrain our freedom. Being put at a relative disadvantage is either actual or in the offing. Unjustified constraint of our autonomy mitigates the danger lying poses to our character by altering the usual context in which virtue (and vice) is displayed or nurtured. It is not disrespectful to prevent another from unwarranted attack on our autonomy; he has already shown disrespect for us. Respecting others hardly demands conspiring in treating ourselves with disrespect. On the contrary, self-respect would seem to demand defending one's autonomy, perhaps by means of a lie.

Before proceeding to the inherent disvalue of self-opposition, it is instructive to note how the lack of respect shown in lying suggests several ways in which lying is distinct from and perhaps distinctively worse than other forms of deception. It may be that lying demonstrates greater disrespect than these sorts of deception or demonstrates it in a particularly insulting way.

First of all, the lie addresses another as a language user. Lying *must* immediately abuse a dimension of human beings that is decisive to their humanity. Charles Fried points out that language is shared and communal in nature. Lying can succeed (as Kant's universalization procedure reveals) only against a backdrop of widespread truthfulness. The disrespect, then, is not merely for the deceived but for mankind in general since the lie trades upon a communal practice and human interdependence. In explicating Kant's claim that a lie, "does wrong to men in general," and "injures humanity," Fried states: "Every lie violates the basic commitment to truth which stands behind the social fact of language."[12] This seems to be true and to help account for our repugnance at lying, but it is not enough to distinguish lying from non-lying linguistic deception.[13]

The social nature of language, however, may provide grounds for such differentiation. Lying is disrespectful to the deceived by being a kind of "treachery." Fried suggests that lying not only attacks the deceived but does so with an instrument (language) that belongs to him. The indignity of being struck with one's own property! But this is also true of linguistic deception in general. In lying, however, the treachery is greater because the deceived is attacked directly and completely with the shared linguistic instrument. Lying offers a complete falsification; the deceived is required simply to accept it passively. What separates lying from other sorts of deception, then, is the non-autonomous posture the dupe suffers.

In both non-linguistic and non-lying linguistic deception, the deceived must actively make an inference from some outward behavior. He is more automonous in the deceiving "transaction." At least some deference is paid to the deceived's autonomy of judgment as he is given some "reasoning room" in which to complete the attack on him; he must be somewhat of an accomplice to the deception process. In lying, however, we abuse language more flagrantly, using it to produce unilaterally and completely the opposite of what we believe true. Perhaps it is the flagrance with which we disrespect the deceived as autonomous language user that lends indignation to the phrase "boldfaced lie." Lying requires a boldness and coldness of purpose in order that we confront the other with a falsehood "complete-in-itself."

In a more pointed consideration of disrespect, Chisholm and Feehan return us to the particular relation between the liar and the deceived. They offer a quick suggestion as to why lying is thought worse than other kinds of deception. The deceived has a right to expect that the liar himself believes what he asserts.

> If a person L *asserts* a proposition p to another person D, then D has the *right to expect* that L himself believes p. And it is assumed that L knows, or at least that he ought to know, that, if he asserts p to D, while believing himself that p is not true, then he violates this right of D's. But analogous assumptions are not made with respect to all other types of intended deception . . . Lying, unlike the other types of intended deception, is essentially a breach of faith.[14]

Violating any right of another's exhibits lack of respect. But if Chisholm and Feehan are correct and lying involves a right with regard to expectation about the liar himself, then the disrespect seems heightened. The liar trades upon a trust placed in him as a speaker. The deceived is encouraged to believe that the liar is revealing his self and this aspect of falsely leading another "into" one's self amplifies the element of disrespect in cases of lying.[15]

Self-Opposition

With consideration of how lies misrepresent the liar's person, we come to the second disvalue inherent in lying: the self-opposition or distancing from the self necessarily generated by repudiating in speech what we believe. Recall that lying always involves intending for the deceived to believe two propositions which are false. One pertains to the specific matter at hand, the other to the liar's beliefs. The deceived has a mistaken belief about what the liar believes, and by extension, who the liar is. But this is to look at the situation from the deceived's viewpoint, rather than to focus on the liar's mental state. By disguising himself from others the liar is perforce put at a distance from who he really is and in opposition to what he really believes.

When we lie we are not "following through" on what we truly believe. Thus, we are separated in action from our beliefs. It is as if the actor were a different person, one acting on a different set of beliefs. The act does not present the real self, for the real self is identified with and by the beliefs held to be true. The beliefs held to be true interlock with the individual's character and conduct in a way that those thought false do not. The beliefs held true by a bigot or saint, for example, are inseparable from her attitudes, dispositions, and actions. Together they define who and what she is. The content of the lie, therefore, is antagonistic to what the individual is.

> A man who lies, in a sense, opposes himself: he denies what he affirms or affirms what he denies. And this is no wrestle of legitimate natural impulses, for there *is* no autonomous impulse to lie.[16]

According to Isenberg, speaking what we believe has a "natural" force. It is simply true of human psychology that there is no "inherent motive force" to make someone else believe what one does not oneself believe. On the other hand, there is a natural (and healthy) transition between belief, thought, and speech. The suggestion is that this natural transition bespeaks a unity or continuity of self which is undermined by lying. When we lie, "the thought that has been naturally prompted by the question is suppressed."[17] The self-opposition, then, is "necessary" to lying because of human psychology and the place of language in it.

Saying something other than what we believe almost always calls for either a reason or an explanation. Saying what one does believe, on the other hand, is not odd. We take "consistency" of this sort for granted, as the norm. "It is absurd to ask why a man who thinks that today is Tuesday should say that today is Tuesday."[18] But what is the weight of this fact and what does it indicate? It indicates that consistency between belief and speech is what a psychologically healthy individual exhibits in the ordinary course of events. Social intercourse and joint activity demand that speech be a rational extension of belief. When speech fails to express what is believed, we reasonably expect either a justification in terms of a reason, or an explanation such as momentary distraction, memory failure, or a more severe disorder.

Now there does exist a reason for saying what one believes, but we typically are not required to have or produce it (extreme situations, when lying may be justified or demanded, however, might in fact require that we produce it). When we say what we do not believe, on the other hand, we should "have" a reason for saying it. It is not enough merely that one exists. "I do not believe it," simply does not carry the weight of an initial reason the way "I believe it" does because of the way we use language.

An inherent end of speech is the communication of belief. On this teleological view, explicating part of what Isenberg means by "natural," lying runs counter to this natural end of language. Kant says that the liar "has a purpose directly opposed to the natural purposiveness of the power of communicating one's thoughts."[19] Since the liar necessarily shares in this "natural purposiveness" of language, he opposes himself by lying. He opposes himself as a language user and as a thinker dependent upon the cogency of his language use. Language is that through which we think, with ourselves as well as others. Lying sets language against the linguistic fabric on which the effectiveness of the liar's thinking depends.

By opposing himself as language user and thinker, the liar thereby opposes himself as an autonomous being. Language use is fundamental to his autonomy of judgment and action. By lying, then, the liar acts in a way that repudiates the conditions necessary for his own autonomous functioning. Because thinking depends upon the shared, social use of language, the liar's self-opposition jeopardizes the coherence of his beliefs and his self-knowledge. Because autonomy depends upon both of these, his self-opposition further jeopardizes his autonomy.

Integration of Opinion and Self-Knowledge

By insulating the liar's beliefs from others, the lie can deepen and enlarge the liar's self-opposition in two ways. It contingently endangers the integration of the liar's beliefs and self-knowledge. Because belief integration and self-knowledge strengthen autonomy, moreover, autonomy is concomitantly jeopardized as well. Lying interrupts social, linguistic processes whereby opinions are integrated and self-knowledge furthered. Lying obstructs the organization of our beliefs and our knowledge of self, first by generating self-opposition and then by shielding it from remedy.

Just as a hovering, interfering parent is an impediment to his child's learning without being either a necessary or sufficient condition for the child's failure, so lying is an impediment to belief integration and self-knowledge. Lying makes more difficult difficult processes by isolating the liar from others. As a result of this isolation, lying separates the liar's beliefs from one another and the liar from himself.

It is commonplace that the liar is often restricted by his lie(s). The lie, to his immediate advantage, often results in an overall net loss of autonomy of action — in what he can do or say.[20] (Consideration of this may include the psychic cost of keeping clear about the tangled web the lies have woven.) The liar must be circumspect in his speech and action, guarding against the emergence of his real beliefs. The need to maintain the deception binds him. The liar's loss of autonomy works from the "outside — in." Limitations on his actions, especially what he is free to say, limit his thinking. This is the inverse of the deceived's loss. For him, autonomy is handicapped from the "inside — out." The limitations on his autonomy of judgment hamper his autonomy of action. The circumstances of the lie limit the way the liar interacts and speaks with others. Because social intercourse is needed to organize our opinions and know ourselves, his social, linguistic isolation obstructs the liar's organization of beliefs and self-knowledge.

A. *Integration of Belief*

Let's consider first how lying jeopardizes integration of opinion. Integration of opinion requires social intercourse. The circumstantial constraints imposed by lying keep the liar from exposing certain of his beliefs. He cannot permit other people to respond to them, yet such response is necessary to their assessment and eventual integration with the rest of the liar's thought. Lying disjoins what is believed from what is said. As a result, what is believed is severed from the integrative process furthered in speech.

To the extent that the individual lacks belief integration, to that extent he is less autonomous. Where restriction of reason limits the deceived's autonomy, for the liar the loss is deeper. The deceived's deliberations (and the actions that depend upon them) are simply skewed or distorted by the lie. But the liar's very ability to deliberate, decide, and act so as to implement decision is threatened by the lie. Belief integration is fundamental to these functions which are constitutive of autonomy. The liar's "efficacy of will" is threatened; in particular, his autonomy of action and the "deliberateness" of his will.

In the first place, the less integrated our beliefs are with one another, the more likely are they to be inconsistent. Inconsistent beliefs make it impossible to have a coherent ranking of values or commitments. We are kept from understanding what we take to be most important to us. Clearly this impedes our second-order autonomy, in particular, that aspect of autonomy of will we termed "deliberateness" (chapter 1, second section, B). We are hindered in our attempt to formulate consistent overarching principles. When faced with a serious situation, therefore, we may be incapacitated from making the crucial decision. With the "core" of our self in disarray, lack of autonomy of judgment hampers our autonomy of action.

Secondly, lack of integration among our beliefs yields inconsistent goals. Among the objects of belief are desires and emotions; therefore, inconsistent beliefs make it more likely that we will be moved emotionally and appetitively in conflicting directions. This inner conflict reduces the deliberateness of our will. We are internally "going in different directions." Consequently, lack of integration among our beliefs makes it difficult to pursue successfully what goals we have (regardless of whether they are scrutinized or not). The courses of action on which we embark are liable to cancel one another. Since our actions arise from our beliefs, beliefs which are at odds with one another will tend to generate actions which don't happily build upon one another. This is a restriction of our autonomy of action.

There is also a more general sense in which lack of integration among our beliefs yields less autonomy. The more our opinions fit together, the less they contradict one another, the more they are "our own." They are more autonomously our own by virtue of forming a unity. Consistency in belief, for better or worse as far as their content, yields oneness of mind, purpose, and direction. This makes for greater autonomy. The notion that integration of belief and personality promotes autonomy is explored more fully in the discussion of privacy in chapter 5.

Here we might add that the less integrated our opinions, the more difficult it is to know what we believe. When our beliefs are connected in a coherent fabric, we more easily see them in relation to one another. Seeing them in relation to one another enables us to understand and appreciate their implications (for action as well as thought), meaning, and relative "weight." When beliefs are not well integrated, we are liable to hold incompatible beliefs and commitments, such as egalitarian as well as racist beliefs. This very incompatibility may easily escape our attention so that we don't really know "what" we believe. Because we are partially defined by what we believe, lack of such knowledge is also lack of self-knowledge. Lack of integration of belief is but one way in which lying jeopardizes the liar's self-knowledge.

B. Self-Knowledge

The isolation of belief from the social world is also an impediment to the liar's self-knowledge. And this, too, undermines his autonomy. Lying is a misrepresentation of who and what we are, a misrepresentation that also seals something of ourselves from others. By disguising ourselves from others, we can easily lose sight of ourselves as well.[21] Lying deprives us of others' response to this closeted part, yet we depend upon their responses to criticize and understand ourselves. Lying conceals the individual's true beliefs from himself by restricting their social disclosure.

Lack of critical self-understanding clearly would limit our second-order autonomy of judgment. Second-order autonomy of judgment involves critical scrutiny of our deepest held values and commitments, and decisions on their retention, revision, or replacement. The less we know ourselves — what we believe and why we believe it — the weaker our position with regard to evaluating and renovating our commitments. Without others' questions, evaluations, and criticisms, we are seriously limited in how well we know our desires and ideals as well. How can we formulate a life-project or ideal of who we wish to be without another's views to press against? Thinking, and the self-understanding that may be its product, is dialectical, requiring another viewpoint off of which to play.

As with integration of opinion, the degree to which self-knowledge is obstructed by lying depends upon the lie's two material conditions: content and situation. The more our lies touch our basic beliefs, values, and commitments, the more the core of our self is likely to elude our critical examination. This results in greater limitations on our second-order autonomy. This is because meta-decisions about these values and commitments will be distorted or deflected altogether. On the other hand, depending on how the lie is situated, the liar may be relatively free to expose his real beliefs. The scope of concealment demanded by the lie determines the degree to which whatever is concealed becomes obscured from us or separated from other beliefs.[22] Variability in the material conditions therefore determines the degree to which the liar is likely to be kept from knowing himself.

But to this it might be objected that lying can actually promote self-knowledge (and thereby self-integration). The practiced, incisive liar, like Shakespeare's Iago, might in fact know himself better than most people know themselves since in order to perpetuate his duplicity he must scrutinize his inclinations, monitor his impulses, and prepare his speech. Robert Audi puts this eloquently: "If one does not know the subjective territory well, one is unlikely to succeed in camouflaging the traces of its buried skeletons."[23] The fact that the effort needed to keep the lie working may in some cases further the liar's self-knowledge does not weaken the claim I am making here, rather, it indirectly (and surprisingly) supports it!

The first thing to notice about the "Iago case" is this: It is precisely because Iago has put himself at a distance from himself by lying that he must work so hard at the self-monitoring which subsequently yields the self-knowledge. This is a favorable outcome of the intial schism inherent in lying. Nevertheless, the general tendency of such divisiveness is to limit self-knowledge, even though an exceptional liar may confront the danger thus posed in a constructive way. Loss of hearing is a force destructive of one's ability to compose music even though an exceptional composer may surmount the obstacle. More analogous might be the individual who insults someone, then establishes a fast bond of friendship in the ensuing effort to make amends. Insulting is, nevertheless, a disturbance which works in the direction of unharmonious further relationship. Precisely because lies obstruct self-knowledge (the way insults obstruct friendship) can the exceptional liar exercise capacities needed to surmount their obstruction. The fact that an impediment or handicap has been overcome does not make it less an impediment or handicap.

In considering the Iago case, we should go a bit further. To what extent is Iago likely to have overcome the opposition to and isolation from self so as to maintain self-knowledge? Iago's real beliefs cannot be examined by others and constructively criticized. The successful self-monitoring liar is still enclosed in a private world. This underscores again the social dimension of second-order autonomy of judgment. We need others to mediate our examination of our basic beliefs and values. Lacking the insights and questioning others can provide, the Iago-like individual is hampered in the self-scrutiny of his fundamental commitments. Ideally we examine ourselves and resolve to be a certain sort of person, in part, through interaction with others.

The last thing to note about the self-knowledge achieved by Iago is its sphere. Iago has become an expert on a narrow portion of himself. Has he not been put at a distance from his love and esteem for Othello? Because of the disrespect for Othello generated, Iago ceases to know that part of himself which was the very spring for the lies. Iago knows himself only within the narrow circumference of his lies. The lies, the subsequent self-monitoring, as well as the circumstantial restrictions, freeze development of further relationships and extinguish the growth of incipient tendencies in the liar. This results in an overall loss of self-knowledge.

The Iago-like liar knows himself primarily as the lies define him. So much more of what he is and could be is lost to the individual because he is lost in a portion of himself. Aspirations, emotions, would-be relationships and projects, all of him that falls beyond the net cast by his lies must be neglected. Another way to put this is to say that Iago does not know himself as potential, as a host of possibilities unconnected to the lies with which he is preoccupied. Human identity includes this potential for acting and being. When it is concealed from us, something of our identity is as well. What Iago knows of himself is therefore, at best, both narrow and static. While he might, indeed, come to know (something of) himself better because of lying, however deep it be, it is knowledge of a limited and limiting facet of his self.

With regard to lack of awareness of self as potential, of possibilities for self-creation, the liar's second-order autonomy is seriously compromised. As we saw in chapter 1, second-order autonomy involves setting out to be a certain sort of person, realizing one cluster of potential character-traits rather than some others. This requires knowing what traits one already has, evaluating them, and projecting an ideal that is feasible. When the liar limits his self-knowledge to a narrow portion of who he already is, he thereby blinds himself to possible features his self could realize. He fails to see ideal selves he could become, or at least desirable traits he could cultivate. In so doing he necessarily reduces the options for the exercise of his second-order autonomy.

I hope that we have seen how and why what is wrong with lying turns on its relationship to autonomy. Attention to autonomy especially enables us to see how deeply lying handicaps the liar, the very one whose interests were suppose to be served by the lie. Understanding the place of autonomy in our lives should also illuminate our caring, nurturing relationships. In the next chapter we will examine the way it informs the parent-child relationship.

CHAPTER FOUR

Parents and Children, Obligation and Friendship

Our treatment of respect obviously leaves us short of deeper, more extensive moral relations with people we are close to. As we have seen, respect at least limits our field of acceptable conduct. But even when it goes further and requires positive action, its demands tend to be minimal. Many personal relationships take us past mere respect, or, the nature of these relationships increases the demands of respect. Family and friendship, for example, involve commitments, obligations, and affection which have serious moral ramifications. While the range of these ramifications is broad, involving much more than just autonomy, autonomy nevertheless figures in their moral story in pivotal ways. In what follows, I shall examine the role of autonomy in the parent-child relationship in particular.

In discussing how autonomy figures in the parent-child relationship, I will focus on two themes. The first concerns the kind of obligations that parents and children have or may come to have toward each other. The nature of the relationship itself creates certain obligations and also provides opportunities for the creation of others. Parents, especially, are in a position to help their children even into adulthood. The second is the issue of friendship as a possible ideal by which parents and their adult children should orient or govern their relationship. Much has been made of this recently, and I would like to take issue with it. I shall argue that the parent-adult child relationship is ideally both more and less than genuine friendship. This entails emphasizing the differences between friendship and the parent-child relationship. Each has important goods that the other doesn't. The large area of overlap which defines the kind of friendship that parents and children can enjoy won't receive much attention. Focusing on the role of autonomy in the parent-child relationship will illuminate questions of both friendship and obligation as they arise in this intimate context.

Part One: Obligations

"Basic" Parental Obligations

The most natural place to begin our examination of obligation and autonomy is with parents' obligations to their children. Parents have what might plausibly be construed as "basic obligations" to care for and help their young. These basic obligations in part arise from the parents' causal roles in bringing their children into the world. Because they are causally responsible for the existence of these beings, parents are obliged to provide them with certain benefits.

But causality alone is not enough to generate moral responsibility. The parent must also act autonomously in playing this causal role. This is because moral responsibility presupposes autonomy. Most obviously, the parent must enjoy autonomy of action, so that someone who is forced to bear a child is not morally responsible for its welfare. But, in addition, autonomy of thought must go into the choice to procreate. Knowledge of the responsibilities of child-rearing is needed, as well as an understanding of the reproductive process and the like. Moreover, a cluster of social practices assigning child-rearing to parents rather than other people or institutions must be in place. The parent must be aware of these practices in order to be functioning autonomously. The issue of autonomous decision-making in general, and with regard to the care of children in particular, raises the

question of societal responsibility for fostering autonomy —
a question we shall not pursue here.

When parents[1] procreate autonomously and the social
institutions assign them the role of rearing their offspring,
then parents have basic obligations to care for their children.
But what are they obliged to provide? They are obliged to
provide the sort of care needed to help their children grow
up to be healthy, secure, and yes — autonomous people. While
autonomy is not the only goal parents ought to strive for, it
is fundamental and related to many others. On the one hand,
several important parental contributions are crucial to the
development of the child's autonomy. The emotional nurtur-
ing parents are obliged to provide is needed for the child to
become autonomous. Further, the self-worth which devolves
upon such nurture is essential to thinking and acting
autonomously. And healthy, educated people obviously have
more opportunities and greater capacity for autonomous
action than those who aren't.

On the other hand, autonomy seems a requisite for other
goods. Autonomous people are better equipped to enter into
strong emotional relationships, such as friendship, since such
relationships require flexibility, critical re-evaluation, and
independence of mind. As we shall see, in an ideal friendship, the parties are equally autonomous. Friendship with
someone with a high degree of autonomy, therefore, requires
commensurate development of the other. In addition,
autonomy is needed for success in all sorts of creative ven-
tures, such as professional vocations and artistic endeavors.
In both professional life and artistic work, the individual must
have independence of mind and the ability to sustain an
original undertaking.

But why are parents obliged to foster autonomy in their
children? The answer lies in the value of autonomy together
with the parents' responsibility for their children's welfare.
As we saw in chapter 2, autonomy obviously has all sorts of
extrinsic value, and a reasonable case can even be made that
it is intrinsically good. Since developing autonomy pretty
much turns on how a child is raised, that burden falls on the
parents. Rather than reiterate the earlier discussion of the

value of autonomy, let's instead pursue the idea of autonomy's extrinsic value as it bears especially on the parental obligation of child-rearing.

A. *Extrinsic Value of Autonomy, Reconsidered*

Among the different kinds of extrinsic value a thing may possess, instrumental value is probably the most common or at least commonly thought of. Autonomy is valuable as the means to realizing all sorts of good things. The more autonomous we are, the more choices or live options we have. Putting the matter in terms of parents and children, Joel Feinberg claims, "the child's right to have his capacity for autonomy developed translates into a 'right to an open future.' "[2] Given the complexity and changeability of the world today, having more options is better than having fewer — to realize whatever values one has, including happiness. Autonomy is also needed to discover valuable things and not simply to pursue those options which present themselves to us. On a deeper level, autonomy is necessary to the re-evaluation of what we currently think is worthwhile.

Children have this right to an open future because of two things. First, because parents are obligated to ensure as best they can that children will grow up to live well. Second, because parents aren't prescient enough to figure out either what a good life for this child would look like or (supposing they were) how to mold the child to realize it. This parallels Mill's utilitarian defense of liberty. Since we can't do a very good job figuring out how others should live so as to maximize their happiness, we should let them decide for themselves how to live. The individual is (usually) in the best position to decide what living well is for him and how to pursue it. By being autonomous the adult child is more likely to know herself and how to match that self with the world's opportunities. The best that parents can do to equip their children to know themselves and make these sorts of decisions is to help them develop into autonomous people. This follows from the parents' limitations and abilities, in conjunction with the plausibility of Mill's hypothesis that the individual is usually in the best position to determine his or her own happiness.

Let me suggest another way to approach this line of justification. Autonomy is the best defense we can give our children against control by others. Autonomy enables the individual to decide for himself on the merits of a view or mode of conduct. Moreover, the autonomous person is more likely to be on the lookout for manipulative techniques and know how to deal with them. The person lacking autonomy is more easily directed by others, with little assurance that this direction will be for his or her own good. There just doesn't seem to be much reason to think that being controlled by others, in general, is going to be good for people. This leads us back to the basic claim that in general people are best off when governing themselves by their own lights. To ensure that their children are not interfered with in this enterprise, therefore, parents should work for their autonomy.

This has yet another implication for parents. Let's imagine that some parents have an idea of what the outlines or foundations of a good life amount to. Let's suppose, as a shorthand, that this is expressed in terms of their values or principles. What assurance do these parents have that their values and principles will be adopted by their children? One alternative is for them to try to indoctrinate their child, "imposing" their values on him and stifling his attempts at critical reflection. Is this the parents' best bet? I don't think so. The child who is indoctrinated may automatically embrace the doctrinal view, but he is unlikely to be able to withstand serious attack on it or doubt arising from within. This approach is likely to yield strong but brittle values and principles. Moreover, some children are apt to reject the very attempt at indoctrination, either out of rebelliousness, peer influence, or educational counter-examples.

The alternative is for parents to raise their children to live autonomously and try to argue for their values and principles. This means offering opposing viewpoints and helping their children criticize them. Of course, this "autonomy-respecting" approach can't be totally without bias. The parental values and principles have the advantage of the child's affection and loyalty to the parents as well as the parents' superior reasoning ability. But we are talking about the "best" that right-minded parents can do to ensure that their values and principles are passed on to their children. And this includes the context of a loving relationship. The best they can do, I offer, is to work for their children's autonomous adoption of these values and principles without taking too much advantage of their privileged rhetorical position. Moreover, to be consistent with this autonomy-respecting approach, the very values and principles which they argue for should be autonomy-affirming, but that is another story (see chapter 1, fifth section).

B. Developing Autonomy

Let's turn our attention more pointedly to the bearing the value of autonomy has on the parent's child-rearing. If Feinberg is correct and the child has a right to an open future (due to parental fallibility, world complexity, or the right to self-governance), then parents are prohibited from doing some things and required to do others. As noted above, parents are prohibited from constricting their children's thinking through indoctrination. Dogmatically inculcating political or religious belief, for instance, inhibits the child's ability to think critically about the view indoctrinated. This includes the ideas and values that fall within the view's scope, such as those which the view excludes. More importantly, indoctrination fosters the habit of uncritical acceptance and rejection — a dogmatic or passive temperament. As suggested above, this leaves the child defenseless should the doctrine fail him or should he lose his conviction in it. He is like a traveller who knows only one route to get where he needs to go. Lacking skill at orienteering or map-reading, he is at a loss should his route be blocked.

Parents are also prohibited from limiting their children's ability to think and choose courses of action by taking over these functions for the child. Quite independent of questions of indoctrination, parents may simply "usurp" their children's prerogatives. In these cases, children are told what to do and their futures are laid out for them as set. As we know, this can be from the most benign motives and children may even find such a life comfortable or secure. But it nonetheless leads to habits of dependence if not helplessness.

On the positive side, the child's right to an open future means that parents have to help provide those educational experiences that foster the ability to think critically and act on the results of this thought. By exposing their children to a variety of perspectives and opinions, for example, parents encourage open, critical thinking. Marilyn Friedman[3] argues that awareness and consideration of diverse points of view enhances autonomy. For one thing, knowledge of this diversity increases the individual's options for thought and action. For another, it keeps the parents' own values and viewpoints in "perspective." Exposure to a variety of viewpoints is clearly an antidote to indoctrination. But it is also a corrective to a more benign, less self-conscious cousin of indoctrination — simple narrowness of mind. By supporting the child's examination of views other than their own, parents enliven their children to a spectrum of ideas and encourage the process of critical reflection.

Parents not only have to help the child develop autonomy, but they have to provide occasions for expressing autonomy and help the child find such occasions. Indeed, one aspect of autonomy is just this ability to seek out, even fabricate opportunities for autonomous living. Autonomy is more than simply being able to react to situations as they are presented. In its fullest development, autonomy includes this ability to ferret out options, seize them, and even devise possible courses of action on one's own. Therefore, parents need to help their children cultivate this kind of initiative rather than content their children merely to react to what is plainly offered.

This means that parents must encourage their children to take risks, to test their capacity for self-governance in settings where the outcome is uncertain.[4] As Dewey (and Aristotle before him) would note, this requires avoiding two extremes: on the one hand, permitting challenges that are likely to overwhelm the child; on the other, protecting the child from all sorts of mishaps at the expense of independence. Parents must aim for demanding challenges that won't leave the child repeatedly frustrated or dispirited. The child needs to succeed in confronting opposition enough to feel confident in her self-governing capacities. Confidence underlies our disposition to take intelligent risks and test our capacities for self-governance.

Obviously, there are many things that parents need to do to help the child feel confident in herself, including provide support, praise, and a good example. Critical here is conveying to the child a sense of worth, of individual value. Elizabeth Newson suggests that, "The crucial characteristic of the parental role is its *partiality* for the individual child; . . . a developing personality *needs* to perceive itself as especially valuable to somebody."[5] Newson argues that in order to perceive herself as especially valuable to the parent, the child must see that the parent will go to unreasonable lengths for her sake. This establishes that the child matters more than others, especially other children. This might include the parent taking great pains to arrange for the child's artistic or athletic development, or helping the child in especially ambitious undertakings. The danger in this is that the parent will do too much for the child and thereby foster dependency.

Of all our relationships, the parent-child relationship seems most liable to dependency. This is probably due both to the child's utter early dependency as well as the deep and complex emotional attractions for the parent of keeping the child dependent. Even if Haworth is correct, and children naturally tend toward autonomy, growth in autonomy usually requires great effort and ability to cope with failure. Consequently, children too may find dependency comforting, for a while. (For an extended discussion of what dependency is and what is wrong with it, see chapter 2, fifth section).

Because autonomy includes the ability to act on one's beliefs in an effort to realize one's ends, parents have to help their children develop discipline. No matter how educated and informed, no matter how capable of independent evaluation and critical thought, a child without self-control is lacking in autonomy. Parents begin by imposing discipline on the child, but this must give way to the child becoming disciplined herself. The capacities for living autonomously develop in stages, some of which are critical for learning how to withstand the promptings of momentary desires and passions.

Of course, there are many other things parents can and should do to promote their children's autonomy. Ensuring that their children enjoy privacy, for example, is pivotal. Privacy plays a fundamental role in the development of the child's sense of self, in particular, her sense of self *as* autonomous. Because it occupies such a central place in the development of autonomy, I treat privacy at greater length in a separate discussion (chapter 5). The details of autonomous rearing need occupy us no further. After all, we are concerned with the broad question of what parents are obliged to do for their children, especially as this pertains to autonomy.

Reciprocal Obligations

So far we can conclude that parents are obliged to do all sorts of good things for their children, especially foster their autonomy. Doing these good things imposes no obligations on their children. This is because in general, people do not incur obligations as the result of receiving benefits which are themselves obligatory. When parents provide benefits that are required by their basic obligations their children are not thereby obligated to reciprocate. From whence, then, do filial obligations to reciprocate arise?

Perhaps children are obliged to recriprocate when parents provide non-obligatory benefits. It is tempting to follow Daniel Callahan's lead here: "It is certainly possible to imagine a sense of obligation arising when parents have done far more for children than would normally be required of them . . ."[6] When parents exceed their basic obligations in providing their children with benefits perhaps the children are then obliged to reciprocate. But, I think that even here the conditions determining reciprocal obligation need narrowing. And this has to do with whether or not the children are able to respond autonomously to their parents' giving.

Suppose parents go beyond their basic obligations by totally dedicating themselves and their resources to the cultivation of their children's intellectual gifts and artistic talents. The children are not obligated by enjoying these extra benefits because they were unrefusable. To the extent that they are unable to refuse benefits, the children are not functioning autonomously. They are not able to make an independent, deliberate choice in the matter. When benefits are thrust upon us, we are not obliged to reciprocate as a result of enjoying them.[7] While most obvious in benefits infants and young children receive, even in adulthood children may not be able to refuse certain benefits. Benefits which are unknown to the child or are "irreversible" fall into this group, as when a parent pays off an unknown debt or leaves a social gathering to spare the child a conflict.

Notice that nothing I've said rules out the importance of children loving or being grateful to their parents for bestowing these extra, though unrefusable, benefits. Perhaps children "ought" in some sense to feel love or gratitude, but that is another matter, and an "ought" which is distinct from the ought of obligation.

What of refusable benefits? Does their receipt oblige children to reciprocate? Sometimes. Again, it depends on the exercise of autonomy as well as the history of the parent-child relationship. If the (non-obligatory) benefit conferred is refusable but nonetheless unrequested, the question of the child's obligation to reciprocate becomes murky and cannot be decided independent of specific details of the situation. The fact that the child could have refused the unrequested help might mean that he is obliged to reciprocate. Accepting the help is an exercise of autonomy and choosing to enjoy the benefit may generate a reciprocal obligation. However, the assistance might also be reasonably construed as a gift, freely bestowed, with no strings. What sorts of details clarify whether the child is obliged to reciprocate refusable but unrequested assistance?

One relevant detail is the nature of the interaction itself: the behavior and attitudes of the parents and children. The child who eagerly accepts the help, opting for more rather than less in the alternatives offered by the parents would seem to obligate himself to reciprocate. On the other hand, the child who graciously turns down the offer of parental assistance, only to accept it at the parent's insistence would seem more the recipient of a gift. After all, gifts are sometimes refusable; therefore, simply accepting a refusable benefit does not automatically entail an obligation to reciprocate.

Also germane is the history of the relationship, including the expectations and conduct of the parents and children. Where there is a history of parents offering unsolicited help and receiving compensation, the expectation of further reciprocation appears warranted. But where parents repeatedly (perhaps adamantly) turn down their children's offer to reciprocate, they may have engendered a tradition of gift-giving. Depending on the history of behavior and the expectations thereby generated, then, children may be obliged to reciprocate when they willingly accept benefits they could have refused.

A clearer situation presents itself when the child receives requested help which the parents are not obliged to provide. The child who asks for money for a down-payment on a house, for example, seems to be obliged to reciprocate. But why is there more clearly an obligation to reciprocate when the benefit is asked for? One explanation is in terms of an implicit understanding or agreement. Help that is solicited implicitly commits the beneficiary to repay the favor should the opportunity arise. The request for help obliges the beneficiary by initiating the other's help. The other is moved to confer a benefit in the belief that the person requesting it is prepared to do likewise.

In support of this idea of "implicit" agreement (usually suspect as an ad hoc rescue), we should note why it remains unspoken. When we agree to help someone, we rarely make explicit the caveat: "If you'll do likewise for me." To articulate the implicit agreement to reciprocate as something like an informal contract might indirectly impugn the other's character, appearing to indicate doubt about his willingness to return favors. This would seem especially true in intimate relationships, such as between parents and children. In a close relationship, how awkward to broach the matter of repayment. Consequently, while an obligation is generated by doing a requested favor for someone with whom we have a strong relationship, we rarely mention it lest we give insult.

When the child incurs a reciprocal obligation, what is she obliged to do? Returning the same favor cannot always be required, if only because useless or impossible — such as sending the parent to medical school. Obviously it is misguided to try for exact answers here, but the notion of providing something of comparable value might yield a rough parameter. What the parent needs may not be money, but effort or time, such as errands run or visits made. The child might best discharge her reciprocal obligation by helping arrange the parent's finances, vacations, or simply the details of daily living. Here, the child may have to be resourceful, for the parent might not ask for help.

This talk of reciprocal obligations between parents and children might provoke the following worry: Doesn't it threaten to reduce the parent-child relationship to one of business transactions or strangers repaying favors? The answer is no, and for two reasons. First, these reciprocal obligations can exist within a larger, loving framework. And, second, because of this larger framework, we ask help from our parents that we wouldn't ask of just anyone. The reciprocity occurs only because housed within a loving relationship. We do not ask just anybody to care for our children, mediate a quarrel, or take us in—just those whom we know and trust and believe have our interests at heart. Moreover, we can't accept help from just anyone. Because we believe that our parents care about us, perhaps in a special way not even friends can, we are able to accept their help. The converse is also true: that parents can ask for and accept help from children that they couldn't or wouldn't from others. We will take up this side of the story shortly, in examining the "humanitarian" obligations children may have toward their parents.

We will now look briefly at two other types of obligations which grown children may have in regard to their parents. The discussion will be cursory because these obligations are not especially concerned with autonomy.

C. Mutual Obligations

In addition to reciprocal obligations, children may also have "mutual" obligations. Jane English argues that mutual obligations arise between friends. She suggests that mutuality is determined by the friend's needs and the other's ability to meet them rather than the balancing of favors rendered against help received. "Friends offer what they can give and accept what they need, without regard for the total amounts of benefits exchanged" (as in reciprocity)."[8] I don't think that children can or should be friends with their parents (as shall be argued presently). However, a loving, friendship-like relationship can ground obligations of mutuality between parents and children.

But why does love or care generate mutual obligations, obligations to help the other without concern for how much has been done in the past? Love, by itself, doesn't create obligations. Why should having an emotion or disposition oblige us? It could be the basis of a duty to ourselves, but that doesn't concern us here. My suggestion is that we might mistake love as the ground of obligation because it is often causally connected to obligation-creating behavior. Love can help generate obligations by motivating behavior which creates strong expectations, beliefs, needs, and emotions. When we show someone a great deal of attention, share intimacies, and make commitments, we alter that person's relation toward us. Because we are responsible for their affection for and reliance on us, we are obliged to do all sorts of things to safeguard and further their good. Instigating these alterations in another's life puts us under obligations that we otherwise would not have. Therefore, while love by itself does not create obligations, the behavior it motivates does.[9]

Now, whatever mutual obligations require of us, they can't require unlimited giving. Surely we are not obliged to do *whatever* it takes to meet a loved one's needs, even if we are able. For one thing, mutual obligations must be balanced against other obligations and interests. For another, beyond a certain level of sacrifice, we are in the realm of the supererogatory, even with loved ones. The limits on what mutuality obliges us to do leaves moral room for both the supererogatory and reciprocity within even the most loving relationship.

Notice that neither mutual nor reciprocal obligations directly depend on how much sacrifice is required in providing the benefit. Need and ability to meet it are the direct determinants of mutual obligations; sacrifice serves only as a limiting factor rather than as the core for determining obligation. Reciprocity could include consideration of sacrifice, I suppose, if the value of the good were to include the cost of providing it. But this doesn't seem right. Benefit enjoyed seems independent of sacrifice needed to provide it. A child's health care, for instance, is the same whether it straps the parent or its cost isn't even noticed. The difference comes in, rather, in terms of the child's response. This involves considerations of character rather than obligation. An adult child "ought" to be grateful to her parents for their willingness to make sacrifices. The adult child "ought" to feel and express such gratitude because that is what children of good character do.

D. Humanitarian Obligations

There is yet a third basis of children's obligations toward their parents. What might be considered our general, "humanitarian" obligation to lend assistance to "anyone" may also hold between parents and children. While this is fairly obvious, it is important to notice how the special parent-child relationship is relevant to discharging this general, non-special obligation. Because parents and children often know one another better than they know most people, and because they may also be in a better position to render help, they sometimes ought to fulfill a portion of their general obligation toward mankind by helping one another. Where acquaintances, less intimate relatives, even friends, may not know what is needed or have the opportunity to do good, children can help their parents precisely because of their special relationship.

We should also bear in mind that parents may be more willing or able to accept help from their children than from others. Because their adult children's help is an expression of the gratitude mentioned above, for example, parents may feel it appropriate, and be comfortable in accepting it. As Daniel Callahan speculates, mightn't the parents' utter dependence on their children create an obligation?[10] It might, especially in light of the children's general humanitarian obligation. Thus, even where mutuality and reciprocity do not oblige children to do something for their parents, their general obligation toward humanity might.[11]

Part Two: Friendship

It is often said by laymen and philosphers alike that ideally children should grow up to be friends with their parents. Growing up and out of the one-sided dependency characteristic of the early phases of their relationship, adult children should become companions to their parents. There ought to be a mutual caring and counsel. This emphasis on friendship reflects the fact that young children become adults able to contribute to their parents' lives in ways comparable to what their parents have done for them. It also reflects the undesirability of the apparent alternatives to friendship: estrangement, continued child-dependence, or mere civility.

Part of the difficulty is that we don't have a word or clear concept to capture the ideal parent-adult child relationship, and "friendship" does indeed come closest to what it should be. How else describe the affection, respect, and give and take into which the relationship should evolve? In what follows, I argue that parents and their adult children cannot become the "true" or "complete" friends they might be with peers. Contrary to an increasingly popular view, it is a mistake to turn to friendship as an ideal by which parents and children should orient or govern their relationships (or philosophers should theorize about them)[12]. Fundamental features of the ideal parent-adult child relationship keep it from developing into full-blown friendship. While peers may fail to become ideal friends, it isn't for the same reasons that parents and their grown children can't. The obstacles between parents and children are built into the structure of the relationship.

On the other hand, parents and adult children can enjoy a relationship rich in qualities that are lacking in the best of friendships. As we shall see, the structural features which prevent complete friendship are also responsible for these goods unique to parents and their adult children. The ideal parent-adult child relationship and complete friendship, therefore, each have valuable dimensions which the other lacks. For the most part, I shall be neglecting the large areas of overlap, areas in which parents and adult children can enjoy a kind of friendship that is quite worthwhile in its own right. I will be purposely pressing the features which differentiate these two important relationships. If my overall contention is correct, one of the things that follows is that the values and virtues of these two relationships are significantly complementary. To have a truly good life, we need both sorts.

Obviously, the following discussion assumes certain parameters to the family structure; however, these wouldn't seem to make the remarks "historical" in a narrow sense. For certain historical periods such as Victorian England, a discussion such as this one would be unnecessary since the very idea of parents and adult children being friends would be laughable. It is precisely in a society such as ours where children have considerable freedom and rights, not to mention power, and where parents too often strive to be youthful, that the idea of their being friends can take hold. In showing that parents and adult children can't be ideal friends even in middle-class America, I do make assumptions which need not hold for all societies.

For one thing, I assume that the parents[13] are primarily responsible for rearing their children. In a society where child-rearing responsibility is diffused throughout the community, as in a Kibbutz, parents and adult children might be able to establish a genuine friendship. In the idealization of the parent-adult child relationship presented here, I also assume that the parents do an excellent job of rearing their children. The thrust of this is that to the extent that parents are ideal parents they cannot enter into an ideal friendship with their grown children. Since my claim is not a logical one it is of course possible for parents and adult children to become ideal friends, just as it is possible to change one's voice pattern or handwriting. However, I hope that the analysis offered here of both the parent-child[14] relationship and ideal friendship relegates that possibility to the merely logical.

Inequality in Autonomy

Parents and adult children cannot become true friends for two reasons. Their relationship lacks the equality friendship requires, and they are not sufficiently independent or separate from one another.[15] Both the inequality and lack of independence from one another result from the distinctive history of the relationship. Let's consider first the sort of equality missing from the ideal parent-child relationship. Aristotle thinks that equally good character is needed in order for true friends to esteem each other sufficiently for equal affection. Only if the friends are equally virtuous will they mutually strive for the other's good for his own sake. Someone who is morally better than another cannot care as much about that person's welfare as he does his own. Moreover, he can't receive enough of the benefits a virtuous friend can provide.[16]

While I agree with Aristotle, inequality in virtue is not the obstacle to friendship between parents and adult children. The inequality which prevents their friendship is inequality in autonomy. By autonomy I mean the ability to be self-determining, to choose for oneself on the basis of one's own values and beliefs. The autonomous person takes into account the opinions and advice of others, but reaches conclusions and decisions based on critical reflection of the matters at hand. Adult children are not necessarily less autonomous than their parents per se, or in general. Rather, they are less autonomous than their parents in the relationship. Although a grown child may generally be more autonomous than her parents, in interaction with them she cannot be. Adult children can't quite "be themselves," at least not all of the selves they've become apart from their parents. Adult children's thoughts and actions are not as free as their parents' *in the context of their relationship*. Moreover, adult children cannot affect their parents in as fundamental ways as parents influenced them when young. This claim about unequal autonomy is what I shall now try to develop and defend. First, let me briefly suggest why equal autonomy is characteristic of true friendship.

Ideal friendship requires equal autonomy in the relationship for several reasons. Without it, there will be unequal influence and power. One friend will be making more of the decisions or having more impact on the decisions at which they mutually arrive. The less autonomous friend will offer less of the resistance and counterpoise upon which the best friendships stay balanced. As a consequence, the friendship of unequal autonomy will tend toward inequality in dependency, with one friend needing or relying disproportionately on the other. The more autonomous party to the relationship will receive less from the friendship, at least in terms of advice, criticism, and alternative perspective. These are important goods inherent to friendship, and their unequal enjoyment is a detriment to complete friendship.

In addition, the lack of equality in autonomy is likely to constrain the mutual and full self-disclosure at work in ideal friendships.[17] The less autonomous friend may be inhibited from revealing too much, lest he become too dependent on the other. The more autonomous friend may be reluctant to confide deeply out of lack of respect for the other friend's judgment or doubts about her willingness to respond with independent conviction. For these and related reasons, equality in autonomy seems ingredient to the best of friendships.

To see why grown children can't be as autonomous as their parents within the relationship we need to examine the unequal exercise of autonomy which characterizes the young child's upbringing. I shall then argue that this history of inequality prevents equality later on, when the child is an adult. The inequality in autonomy has two particularly powerful expressions — one ontological, the other epistemological. To begin with, we should make much of the obvious — the parent helps shape who and what the young child is. Where the parent developed into an adult independently of the child, the young child grows up under the parent's influence and care. The physical, psychological, and social dependence of the child translates into an ontological inequality; the parent simply is more responsible for the being or identity of the young child than the other way around. Bringing the child into the world, raising her, taking part in her successes and failures, the parent contributes to the young child's identity in ways which she cannot reciprocate. While the parent may be changed dramatically as a result of rearing a child, the parent is not shaped by the child. The parent authors change in the young child, exerting control, both intentional and unwitting, over her development.

Who the young child is, then, results in part from the parent's exercise of autonomy. Even the young child's character and degree of autonomy itself ideally are cultivated by parental industry. Their history together is a history of parents making decisions for the young child, provisionally exercising an autonomy on her behalf that the child will (should) eventually exercise for herself.

Two senses of "exercising autonomy" should be distinguished here. The weak sense indicates parents making their own decisions in rearing the young child. Their wishes and decisions with regard to the young child take precedence, and the child must respond to them. This means that the parents are "in charge," able to determine the young child's life in ways that the child is not. The strong sense of "exercising autonomy" indicates that parents deliberately and effectively shape the young child according to their goals for her. We might say that this is a more directed exercise of autonomy, exerted purposefully over the young child's nature rather than simply exerted over her. While the strong sense of "exercising autonomy" in rearing the young child no doubt contributes to a deeper inequality in autonomy, the more typical weak sense is enough to keep parents and adult children from the equality of autonomy needed for friendship.

There is another, obvious feature of the parent-child relationship that we shouldn't overlook. "Real" friends are free to choose one another in a way not open to children with regard to their parents. The fact that we exercise autonomy in choosing our friends, in establishing the relationship, carries over into the relationship itself. We exercise more autonomy in the friendship with peers, especially in defining the relationship, than we do with our parents. And while parents do not choose to have this or that particular child (save insofar as they are able to exercise autonomy in the strong sense), they do choose to have *a* child in a way that children do not choose to have parents.

The inequality in autonomy between parent and young child has an epistemological dimension as well as an onto-logical one. The parent witnesses the young child's coming-to-be. Consequently, he possesses intimate knowledge of the young child's development, including knowledge of the child before she knows herself. This gives the parent special access to the young child's personal identity which the child does not and can never enjoy with respect to the parent. The parent is, literally, an "authority" on the child, at least her child-hood. When the young child is old enough to realize it, she knows that this person enjoys a unique knowledge of her. Perhaps out of the desire for both self-knowledge and reduc-tion in the vulnerability that comes with the parent's superior knowledge, young children typically ask to hear stories about themselves from these pre-reflective days. This epistem-ological disparity complements the ontological inequality in giving the parents greater autonomy in relation to the young child.

Ongoing Inequality

A. *Grown Children*

But why must this history of unequal autonomy in the relationship prevent equality later on, when the child is grown up? It is because this history endures in the identities of the parent and adult child in at least two ways: in their self-concepts, and in their habits and attitudes toward each other.

The adult child's self-concept includes diverse aspects of her history with the parent. The parent protecting, nurtur-ing, encouraging, and letting go all figure in. Our degree of autonomy in general depends upon our self-concept. For example, people who see themselves as able to carry out choices effectively or who have strong body images, tend to exercise greater control over their lives than those who do not.[18] Because it includes the history of the unequal relationship with the parent, the adult child's self-concept limits the degree to which she can function autonomously with the parent.

It might be objected here that such a self-concept reflects an immature adult child suffering from a pathological dependency on the parent. Plagued by memories of parental control, the grown child simply has not outgrown the infantile sense of inferiority. The role I ascribe to the history of the unequal exercise of autonomy, however, is not confined to adult children who can't grow up. Ideally, the adult child's self-concept includes those abilities and competencies the parent was instrumental in cultivating. The self-concept of the healthy, mature adult child has a place for the parent as one who has helped make her autonomous. As such, the parent should (in the best of cases) be seen as a moral authority: teaching right and wrong; exemplifying virtues; displaying moral judgment in helping the young child through quandaries and conflicts. Even some of the values and principles which enter into our self-concept emerge from the history of a healthy interaction between parent and young child. They too will bear the stamp of their parental origin.

The effect of the interaction between parent and young child on the adult child's self-concept is not reducible simply to the memory of dependency. The specifics of the history of unequal autonomy need not be remembered in order to influence the child's self-concept. To illustrate this general point about the formation of self-concept, let's consider cases which don't bear as directly on autonomy.[19] Consider for example the way cultural forces shape our self-concept. In some cultures a person's sense of self is fundamentally determined by kin or clan membership. In contrast, individualistic societies define the self more by personal accomplishment. In neither case must the individual remember the forces of identity-formation for them to condition her self-concept.

The history of the unequal autonomy effects the adult child in another way, besides informing her self-concept. The unequal interactions characteristic of the earlier stages in the parent-child relationship foster habits and attitudes which persist into the child's adulthood. Such attitudes as respect and loyalty, as well as habits of deference and accommodation engendered in youth continue into adulthood. As a result, the adult child is less likely than her parent to press disagreements or criticism in their interaction; she is less likely to assert herself.

Because they receive continuous reinforcement in the ongoing interactions with parents, such basic habits and attitudes are self-perpetuating. Instigated by interaction, these habits and attitudes then beget the consonant behavior, which in turn further entrenches them. Of course, it may be possible to break the habits, dismantle our attitudes towards our parents, even rearrange our self-concept. But not without rebuilding our very selves. The self-concept together with these habits and attitudes critically define who we are.

B. Parents

What has been said about the impact of unequal autonomy on the self-concept, habits, and attitudes of grown children reciprocally holds for parents as well. The parent's sense of self is informed in a complementary way by the history of unequal autonomy. The parent sees himself as provider and protector, teacher and guardian of the young child. Most people include the role of "parent" (but not child) in their self-concept. For it is, after all, something of an occupation: an arduous, rewarding job that becomes part of our self-understanding. A large component of this self-concept hinges on the ontological and epistemological discrepancy discussed above.

The parent sees himself as partly responsible for the adult child's existence, growth, and well-being. He can reasonably take credit for some of her accomplishments as well as blame for various shortcomings. His epistemic superiority also enters into the parent's self-understanding. He is an expert on the formation of his adult child's temperament and tastes, aspirations and humiliations. The adult child, of course, knows that this particular individual (however much a "friend"), unlike all others, knew her and knew all about her before she had consciousness of herself as a person. Perhaps, in addition, the grown child is aware of the parent's self-regard as parent (as constituted along the lines just sketched).

There is an irony in the parent's superior knowledge of the young child; too often it limits parental appreciation of the adult child — even in ideal relationships. Precisely because parents know their children so well as children they may be kept from truly seeing and appreciating who the child is as an adult, the image of the young child coloring the parent's later perceptions. Parents may overestimate the impact on the adult child of certain childhood successes or failures, strengths or liabilities. A poor childhood showing in mathematics, for example, may make it difficult for a parent to accept the adult child's achievements in computer programming. Conversely, a parent may be disconcerted by his adult child's failure to pursue a youthful interest in art or music. It is hard for even the best of parents to shed the recollections of their young child's tastes and proclivities. People who meet us as adults, however, can more readily appreciate who and what we are since unencumbered by childhood history or their role in who we've become. The parties' autonomous histories make possible the equal exercise of autonomy essential to friendship.

As a result of interacting with the young children, parents also develop characteristic habits and attitudes. Such habits as solicitousness and helpfulness, as well as attitudes of concern and protectiveness live on in interactions with their grown children. While children should outlive their childhoods, they remain their parents' children. Even though the original habits and attitudes parents develop in regard to their young children should be modified as the children mature, they are rooted in an inequality in autonomy which is all but ineradicable. Consequently, parents are more autonomous in relation to their grown children, and this inequality keeps them from becoming complete or true friends.

Before examining the second obstacle to friendship, lack of separateness, it may be helpful to consider a few of the ways in which inequality in autonomy is revealed in everyday life.

C. Examples

How does the inequality in autonomy between parents and their adult children manifest itself in less than complete friendship? A few examples of behavior that is appropriate in a peer friendship but not for a parent in relation to his grown child should vivify the position being advanced. Consider a parent complaining to his grown child about the other parent; telling sexual stories or jokes; or, an unmarried parent going with the adult child to socialize with others in sexually oriented ways. While usually acceptable in a peer friendship, these sorts of behavior seem somehow out of place in the parent-adult child relationship. But why?

The answer has to do with the authority enjoyed by the parent. As the "author of his being," the young child's parent possesses an authority over her which does not just disappear once the child is grown up. The parent is ideally a moral authority for the young child: one to whom the child looks for insight and advice. And this, too, is likely to carry over into the child's adulthood.[20] In addition, the parent possesses *de facto* authority — influence or power to secure compliance — as a diffuse consequence of the inequality in autonomy. Due to both sorts of authority parental values and opinions carry disproportionate weight even when meeting filial disagreement. The adult child cannot act as freely in the presence of parents as she can with others. Parental authority, for example, inhibits grown children from expressing conflicting views or criticizing those of the parents. The uncanny ability of parents to constrain or convince, frustrate or exasperate their children well into their adulthood evidences the sorts of authority ascribed to them here. But authority works in different ways to account for what is wrong in the examples mentioned above.

When one parent complains about the other to the adult child, for instance, the second parent's status and authority as parent is jeopardized. If it were just a matter of weakening the other parent's de facto authority (henceforth, simply "power"), the critical behavior might not be wrong. But when the criticism undermines the other parent's credibility as a moral authority (simply "authority"), it seems untoward. The complaining parent seems to be trying to make the child an ally against the other parent. This is likely to make the adult child feel guilty or at least tentative about her relationship with the criticized parent. The adult child's loyalties threaten to be divided: which parent to credit or side with or talk to? If she feels awkward in confronting the criticized parent about the matter, these conflicts may go unresolved for some time. The complaining might also make the adult child feel responsible, either to do something about the conflict or for the existence of the conflict in the first place. For these reasons, the adult child's autonomy is to some extent compromised. Divided loyalty, guilt, and confusion easily impede the adult child's ability to interact freely with the criticized parent.

The critical parent misuses his power and abuses his authority by compromising both the other parent's authority and the adult child's autonomy. This employment of power and authority is especially difficult for the grown child to recognize because it appears to elevate her to the level of peer — as someone fit to judge the other parent. The child is being subtly told that she is the parents' moral equal. But this message conflicts with both the complaining parent's power and authority as well as the now threatened authority of the maligned parent. The authority of the criticized parent is still at work, accounting for the adult child's confusion and mixed feelings. It is ironic that the thrust of this apparently equalizing behavior is to inhibit the adult child's autonomy in interacting with the criticized parent. Such inhibition bespeaks a reduced rather than elevated status. It is just this tension between the appearance of equality and the reality of inequality, responsible for this irony, which accounts for the wrongness in the next two examples.

In both sexual banter and socializing, there is an apparent renunciation of parental authority. This can cause the adult child conflict in either of two opposite ways, depending on whether the parental authority or the camaraderie predominates. First, because the parent is nonetheless an authority, there is the imposition of parental values which interferes with the adult child's autonomous expression of herself. The adult child naturally feels deference toward or hemmed in

by someone who has raised her. What results is a tension between the buddy-like behavior (with perhaps an undercurrent
of "peer" competitiveness in the case of sexual socializing)
and the parent's implicit authority. With genuine peers,
however, the adult child's autonomy is not restricted, as no
special deference or constraint is dictated by the nature of
the relationship. The adult child is thus free to engage in sexual banter or socializing as she sees fit.

On the other hand, the adult child may be discomfited
by the parent's seeming renunciation of authority, by his step-
ping out of the role of parent. Why else is striving to be "one
of the boys" or "girls" in dress, speech, or behavior so
embarrassing? It isn't just a matter of age. I suggest that it
has to do with the conflict between the embarrassing behavior
and the parent's role.

If my earlier contentions are correct, the parent's role in
rearing the young child leaves a profound residue in the grown
child's persona and interaction with the parent. The parent's
role places his or her sexual activity in a family context. After
all, the parent's sexuality is realized within the family in the
person of the child; the child herself embodies the parental
union. When the parent, even though no longer married,
engages in sexually oriented socializing, his or her role as
parent is clouded. The parent's sexuality is isolated from
family relationships and responsibility. Simply knowing of
this behavior might disturb the grown child. But if the adult
child is actually accompanying the parent in the socializing,
then the child is implicated in the behavior as a witness and
accomplice. She is then likely to feel conflict or resentment
over her parent's refusal to act "like a parent" with her.

Perhaps sexual examples are most apt or spring most
readily to mind because one important way an adult child
demonstrates maturation and emancipation from the parent
is in her own sexual activity. This may be partly due to the
connection of sex with the adult child's emergence into the
role, herself, of parent and householder, independent and on
her own. When the parent steps into the adult child's sexual
world as a cohort, narratively (as in storytelling) or literally
(as in bar-hopping), either the adult child's autonomy is

limited or the camaraderie undermines the parent's status as a moral authority for the adult child.

Lack of Independence

Let us now take up the second obstacle to complete friendship between parents and grown children: their lack of independence from one another.[21] The parent and grown child cannot enter into the relationship as equally developed people, bringing to the relationship the independent histories that fuel and provide a healthy tautness to friendship. Where above we focused on the adult child's lack of autonomy in interacting with the parent, here the parent and grown child lack autonomy from one another: a lack of relational autonomy in the sense of independence from one another.

Neither the parent nor the adult child can meet or view the other as truly "other." To begin with, the union between infant and parent is primitive in the sense of primal. Theirs is an intimacy which begins on a pre-conscious level for the infant, and continues on both a conscious and subconscious level for both parent and child. They experience a pre-verbal and nonverbal sensuous bond, the intimacy of immediate, sensory communication. I suggest that this primitive union persists for both into the child's adulthood.

The young child grows up by means of the parent's help, in the shade of parental direction and protection. From earliest memory, the parent was "there." Much of the way the young child comes to understand herself and world is through her parent's eyes. They shape and color what the young child takes to be important or trivial, noble or banal. Moreover, this influence doesn't just disappear when the child reaches adulthood. Parental tastes and values, opinions and principles, inform the grown child's outlook. In addition, most of us can attest to seeing our parents physically in ourselves: their expressions, gestures, and physical features. Even when not fully cognizant of this continuity and resemblance, they work to unite parent and child.

On the other hand, a sizable portion of the parent's adult life is spent raising his young child. The energy and attention bestowed upon their young children, as much as genetic material, encourages parents to see themselves "objectified" in their children as they become adults. The parent's own identity is bound up in and with his adult child's life. As noted earlier, parents identify themselves *as* parents, like an occupation or religion. The parent is reflected in the adult child, the child a temporal extension of him. Seeing ourselves in our children, love of them is to some extent self-love (so argues Aristotle). Even though the parent is formed independently of the child, much of his identity is nonetheless tied to the adult child's.

Part of the delight in a complete friendship turns upon the way two people discover and grow into each other's lives, but parents and adult children cannot develop in quite this fresh way because their lives have been entwined since the child's beginning. Neither one can really "discover" an independently existing other. They are virtually too close to have the independence needed for friendship. Here it is not a matter of the independence of autonomy, of self-determination. Rather, it is the independence of identity. The union which characterizes true friendship presupposes separateness. Only the truly separate are capable of overcoming their separateness while yet remaining "other." The parent-adult child union precludes the degree of separateness needed.

I am not suggesting a persisting symbiotic relationship in which the participants really have a hard time seeing each other as separate. Each must see the other with needs, interests, and a life of her own. In the ideal relationship, the parent gradually lets go and the adult child finally fends for herself. However, although they may discover particular things about one another as they go their separate ways, neither brings the wholly separate baggage to the relationship the way friends do. As a result they don't discover each other as beings with independent histories and different values to be learned.[22] As a result, parents and adult children don't encounter one another as sufficiently different.

The intimacy we ought to enjoy with our parents keeps us too close. Not in a sick loss of identity or independence, but in the enmeshing of lived life: meals taken, plans hatched, disappointments suffered. Ours is a common history peopled with crises, stories, and other family members — all along, right from the child's beginning. Intimacy and love, sharing and caring, aren't won or earned between parents and children. They evolve. But they are earned with friends. Establishing and maintaining friendships are achievements at which we must work. We prove ourselves before and to prospective friends. We woo them.

A couple of analogies should clarify the sense of otherness I find lacking in the ideal parent-child relationship. Think of your home town. It is part of you, helps constitute you (and you it). You can still view it as separate from you, but not the way you do a new city, where you must forge a home. Or, consider the difference between learning a foreign language and discovering more about your own. We must work to make a foreign language familiar. On the other hand, the way we think of the world, envision the future, deliberate — all are conditioned by our native tongue in a unique way. And so are we formed by our parents as well. They are naturally familiar, like a first language; and we are naturally at home with them, as with our home town.

Valuable and Unique Qualities

If the ideal parent-adult child relationship is less than a full-blown friendship so does it also contain valuable qualities which are missing from friendship. The very conditions which stand in the way of complete friendship (lack of independence from one another and inequality in autonomy) also enable the parent-adult child relationship to be uniquely fulfilling. These rewards, therefore, complement those inherent in true friendship. Let's begin with what we were just discussing: the lack of separateness between parents and children. Viewed positively, this can be construed as "identification."

A. Identification

By "identification" I mean feeling and thinking of another as part of one's self. Who we are is partly defined not just by our relationship to this person, but by the person's life itself. The other's well-being and suffering is experienced as constitutive of our own well-being and suffering. This is more than taking a keen interest in another's affairs. When we "identify" with movie stars or ballplayers, to take popular examples, we share in their triumphs and defeats. The particulars of their lives enrich our own as we see ourselves insinuated in their undertakngs. This sketchy sense of identification will be fleshed out in discussing the way identification animates the parent-adult child relationship.

The parent-adult child relationship involves mutual identification; however, it seems fairly clear that parents identify more with their children. This is probably due to the parents' role in shaping their children's natures. In what follows, therefore, the focus will be on the effect on both parent and adult child of the parent's identification with the child. To the extent that the adult child does identify with the parent, the pattern developed here would then naturally apply in that direction as well.

Granted, then, is the existence of this identification between parents and adult children. How does it add a valuable quality to their relationship which is lacking between friends? Because of their mutual identification, parents and adult children experience a "doubling" of the adult child's fortunes. Parents rejoice doubly in their grown children's success or good luck. They are glad for the adult child but also for themselves, as if their own good. Their adult children are seen as the parents' representatives in the world, the children's successes and setbacks, redounding to the parents' credit or shortcomings. Parents bask in a kind of reflected success the way a coach partakes of her athlete's victory or an editor his writer's triumph. Even some of the parents' self-esteem may be bound up in their grown children's accomplishments or the lack of them. It makes sense to speak of parents taking pride in their children in a way that it doesn't for friends. Friends simply don't take this kind of personal pride in one another's success. Of course they are glad for one another and receive pleasure. But this doesn't seem like parental pride or joy, either in magnitude or kind — the kind that turns on identification.[23]

When perverse, the parent's vicarious delight in the adult child's welfare is extreme, supplanting the parent's interest in his own separate life. But I see nothing untoward in the notion of a "healthy" vicarious enjoyment, one which is borne of the parent's identifying with the grown child. The key is that the vicariousness and identification are limited, kept in perspective, and don't threaten either the parent's regard for himself as independent or the adult child's freedom to go her own way.

At the same time, the adult child takes delight in bringing parents joy through her accomplishments. The adult child's enjoyment is thereby also doubled. To the joy for herself is added the joy of bringing happiness to her parents. She "offers" her accomplishments and herself as something of a gift for the parents to relish. (This will be connected to the special sort of gratitude grown children ideally feel with regard to their parents.) Friends don't seem to regard their success as quite this source of joy for one another. Because friends don't *give* one another great delight by virtue of their own accomplishments, they can't savor their accomplishments as the source of such delight.

The identification between parents and their grown children is also the basis for a negative sort of "doubling." This unpleasant doubling, in itself, probably doesn't enhance the relationship. However, it is worth examining because its presence attests to the strength of the identification which is responsible for the desirable duplication. When adult children suffer failure or bad fortune, their parents anguish doubly. They are sorry for their adult children but also suffer on their behalf the way friends don't. Parents take on their grown children's loss or disappointment. Perhaps this echoes parental empathy for their young children when they were sick or emotionally distraught.

On the other hand, an adult child's unhappiness over her own misfortune extends beyond her self to the sadness it brings her parents. Of course friends grieve with us, as Aristotle says, but parents don't just grieve with us; they also grieve for us. Maybe that is the difference. Friends are with us, consoling and restoring our confidence or hope. But while parents also offer support, they need consoling themselves (which *their* friends, in turn, provide). This is why grown children don't confide certain unpleasant things to their parents. Not necessarily out of distrust, but to spare them the distress such news is likely to cause. Because friends don't need such protecting, we confide more readily in them.

I think that the difference between parents and friends with regard to this "doubling" effect of identification is underscored by the example of grandchildren. Grandchildren obviously bring joy directly to the grandparents. But grandparents also delight in their adult children's own enjoyment of these grandchildren. Grown children, in turn, take great joy in "presenting" their parents with grandchildren, and enjoy their parents' enjoyment of these children. This just doesn't seem a plausible part of the structure of friendship. Friends certainly can enjoy one another's children and become very close to them. But they don't have the kind of vested interest in their welfare that grandparents do. We neither delight in our friends' children the way the children's grandparents do, nor do we take such great pleasure in our friends' enjoyment of their children. The difference between friends and parents with regard to our children is especially brought out in the case of misfortune.

Consider a young child who is severely mentally and physically disabled in an accident. The grandparents suffer twice over, for their own loss as well as their adult child's loss of a normal child. The grief that the parents feel is also felt by the grandparents as a chronic ache, part of their permanent psychology. No matter how compassionate and caring friends are, they are outside the tragedy. It is not "their" child. As a result, they are sad for their friend, but the friend's sadness is not quite their own. Their lives are in a certain sense in tact, apart from the tragedy in a way that the grandparents' are not.[24]

B. Characteristic Love

The parent-adult child relationship is also uniquely enriched by its characteristic types of love and their attendant qualities. The love between parents and their adult children is not necessarily better than that between friends, just importantly different from it. Perhaps because of the sense of their grown children as an extension of themselves, parents (ideally) feel an "unconditional" love for their children: a love that is untouched by accomplishments or failure, kindness or callousness. A love with no strings, which embraces the child's sheer existence even as an adult. Of course parents want their children to do well and are apt to feel pride, admiration, even a species of respect for the adult children when they do terrific things. But these sentiments are over and above the sort of love I am thinking about. Parental love doesn't depend on special achievements or attributes, only on the special connection with the parent.[25]

One way this unconditional love is exhibited is through parents' solicitousness of their children. Persisting through the adult child's life, parental concern for the child is communicated as a readiness to help. As a result, both parents and grown children ideally view the parents' assistance not as an onus to be endured by the parents, but as a generous extension of the succor they provided when the child was young. Within limits, parents like continuing to be a source of wisdom and support. Because they feel the parents' love as unconditional, children may be able to request and accept help from parents that they can't from friends. Granted that we ask favors from friends we won't from our parents, surely we also feel more comfortable turning to our parents for certain *sorts* of help. Most plausible is the help that seems to be an extension of their role as nurturer and provider, such as nursing the adult child through an illness or lending her a substantial amount of money.

The adult child's love for her parent is, in the ideal, not quite this unconditional sort. The adult child's love is built on that primitive intimacy and attachment of which we earlier spoke. Affection naturally flows from and returns to this bond. This affectionate attachment is the basis for the more consciously motivated love that the young child comes to feel. Loving our parents involves loving a protecting, nurturing, unconditionally *loving* authority. Even though the adult child should need less parental protection and nurturance, these qualities continue to define the object of her love. It is a love for an unequal, for one who took care of us and did so gladly. We love those who make us secure, and to the extent that our parents love us unconditionally as adults, we are also secure in that love.

An adult child's love for her parents is grounded in a particular kind of gratitude. Doubtless, the love and care we receive from our parents engenders a gratitude which is at first unreflective, one which grows up with us. A more reflective gratitude involves recognition of all the good things our parents have done for us, including the nurturance and love just mentioned. I think that this gratitude develops most fully out of reflection on our self-love. Just as the parent's love for the child extends his self-love, so is the child's gratitude-filled love for the parent a *product* of her self-love. Because we love ourselves, we love our parents for helping us be worth loving. We give credit to our parents for our good character, our loving nature, our ability to function autonomously. In appreciating ourselves we ideally come to appreciate our parents' contribution to who and what we are. This appreciation takes the form of gratitude-love.

Gratitude per se does not bespeak an enriched relationship. We could be grateful to someone without having much of a relationship with that person at all. A stranger who saved our life at great cost to herself, for example, would have our undying gratitude but our relationship could be rather minimal. A few things should be noted, however, given the context of our discussion of filial gratitude. We are not grateful to our parents for an isolated act or benefit. Rather, we are grateful for the history of interaction and their love which has contributed to our very nature. We may be grateful to our friends for any number of things they do for us. The point is that they can do any number of things for us. But whatever anyone does for us in a sense depends on what our parents have done and are. They have played a fundamental role in making us the people for whom these other things were done. Consequently, our gratitude to our parents abides and resurfaces in other grateful moments.

This points to the fact that our parents' contribution is unique. Only they could make us secure and loving enough, for example, to form good friendships in the first place. We are grateful to our parents for what no one else in principle can do. And this makes the love informed by that gratitude of a different stripe altogether. Unlike our love of friends, the love we have for our parents is grounded in gratitude. There may be more to an adult child's love for her parents, for instance, she may love them for such virtues as patience or wit. But it is the gratitude for helping shape our identities that I am calling attention to here, because that is what distinguishes love for parents most sharply from friendship love.

In the first place, then, the gratitude we (ideally) feel for our parents informs our love for them and this particular sort of love does indeed add to the parent-adult child relationship. In the second place, the gratitude-love we feel toward our parents is expressed in concrete ways and this expression also enriches the relationship. Gratitude for who and what we are is shown differently than gratitude for this or that particular act, or even gratitude for a friendship as such. For example, we may express or exhibit this gratitude indirectly, by striving to realize our natural gifts in the knowledge that this will be especially rewarding to our parents. Since they helped define and cultivate our nature, continuing this growth is especailly appropriate.

Gratitude-love can also be more directly expressed toward our parents. Because they are so responsible for who we are, it is fitting for us to take care of them. While we may also take care of friends, even out of gratitude, this taking care does not mirror what they did for us the way taking care of our parents does. It is not structurally part of the relationship. As a result, it is contingently connected to the friendship in a way that taking care of our parents is not. Taking care of our parents returns us to our origins in a way that friendship nurturance cannot. In this return to our origins we return to our parents as only we can: returning their unconditional love which nurtured us with our gratitude-love. Only we their children can repay them in this way; their friends cannot do this. We shall take up the aesthetics of this parental nurture presently.

There is one more way in which the love between parents and grown children enriches the relationship in a unique way. Our parents' unconditional love for us is irreplaceable. No one else, even the best of friends, can love us the way our parents do. And even though particular friends cannot be replaced, the love which friends are capable of can be had again, with new friends. When our parents die they take their special love with them. In our more reflective moments we anticipate losing this love, since our parents are older. I suggest that both the anticipation and the actual experience of losing our parents' irreplaceable love imbues the parent-adult child relationship with a valuable quality. It bestows a poignancy which prompts us to feel the magnitude of this love's value. Appreciating the full value of our parents' love deepens our overall capacity to feel and appreciate. It increases our depth as people, and this is worth having.

C. Permanence of Status

The parent-adult child relationship has a solidity and stability which derives from the permanence of one's status as parent and child. We outgrow childhood, but not being someone's child. No matter how their functions and needs shift, so that the parent may be taken care of by the grown child, he is still the parent. The status endures, even if many of the specific role functions do not. Friendship is different. We can acquire and lose friends; the status of friend is not permanent for the lives of the parties.

The permanence of status adds a forward-looking dimension to the relationship. Just as the parents and grown children share the history of the young child's life, and know that they do, so do they also see the relationship (whatever its perturbations) as inevitably stretching into the future. They are in it for the "long haul." Of course, when the relationship is seriously lacking, the parties feel this as a burden, something to be endured. But in the ideal relationship, it provides a backbone of durability.

The stability and strength which comes from the permanence of status is buttressed by the lack of choice concerning that status. As remarked earlier, children obviously choose neither their parents nor to be anyone's children. The "giveness" of the relationship for children is all but absolute. It is less so for parents since they (ideally) choose to have children; however, they don't choose to have just these children. We might then say that parents choose to create the relationship, but have only limited choice and control over who is party to it. This clearly contrasts with friendship, in which parents and adult children exercise considerable choice and control. The lack of choice over the relationship qualifies the identification between parents and adult children. The identification is ineluctable, something to be accepted as part of one's lot — unlike identification with role models or professions, which we may freely adopt.

I suggest that the permanence of status, supplemented by lack of choice, adds security for both parties. We are vouched safe against the changes that can beset even the best of friendships, changes that partly hinge on the fact that friendship is so keenly owing to choice. For that reason alone friendship is exposed. For example, parents and adult children as well as friends may have to make a great effort to keep their respective relationships strong during extended periods of separation. However, the permanence or irrevocability of the parent-adult child status provides an impetus for "keeping up." It is harder to let the relationship unravel knowing that this is still your parent, this is still your child.

Obviously, there are important values in relationships which are autonomously entered into and maintained, some of which elude the parent-adult child relationship. What I am claiming here is that these values harbor corresponding risks or drawbacks. The parent-adult child relationship is protected against these liabilities by the very lack of control and choice enjoyed, for example, by friends. Thus, while we may be closer to some friends than to our parents or grown children, and surely love more intensely in romantic love, friendship is more vulnerable because subject to choice and control.

The security found in the parent-adult child relationship is enhanced by the kinds of love which characterize it. Knowing that there is someone who loves them unconditionally surely affords adult children comfort against the turbulence of the love which defines some other relationships. The quiet, steadfast love of our parents provides an appropriate ballast against passionate currents of romantic love, for example. For parents, their adult children's gratitude-love provides a similar surety against the vicissitudes of aging and the loss of peer friendships.

D. Aesthetic Closure

The historical core of the parent-child relationship is, finally, expressed aesthetically. This aesthetic expression enriches the relationship in a unique way. I have in mind two types of aesthetic closure which can characterize a parent-adult child relationship as no other. The first might be considered "cyclical," and the second, the closure of "nexus."

As they age, parents usually come to depend more and more on their adult children for a variety of assistance. While friends also depend on each other, the reversal or exchange of roles in the parent-child relationship adds a basic aesthetic dimension to this dependence. To nurse or bathe or feed in his old age the person who did this for us in our infancy cuts to the heart of our identity. To play the parent to our parents is to complete a human cycle. From the adult child's standpoint, she is incorporating in herself her own childhood by taking care of the person who nurtured her. When this involves helping our parents round out their lives and die, the cycle is truly completed by reversing the way they helped us begin life.

From the parent's standpoint, the adult child represents a regeneration or recreation of the parent as parent. The parent can witness this simply in his adult child's relationship with grandchildren. However, when his adult child cares for him, the parent directly experiences his child in the role of parent. As such, the adult child may exhibit some of the very virtues the parent helped cultivate, only now the parent experiences their benefits first-hand. In a sense, the parent returns to care for himself, externalized and embodied in his adult child. In Aristotelian terms, the craftsman's product is plying the craft on the craftsman himself.

The closure of nexus occurs when a grown child has children of her own. She is then poised between her parents and children. For a time, the grown child is simultaneously child and parent, embodying both. This bringing together of both roles, with the concomittant interactions and emotions discussed above, carries with it a closure different from the cyclical sort. This is the closure of embodying two poles simultaneously, being the locus of an intersection.

When this happens, we mediate the relationship between our parents and children.[26] The relation of each to the other is conditioned by us. This yields the closure of participating in and maintaining a continuity. We are the link between our children and parents, making their relationship possible. We experience ourselves not merely as a nexus, but as a participating nexus. The sense of aesthetic completeness this affords is also foreign to friendship. Even when we are responsible for bringing two of our friends together, it is different. We are not simultaneously playing two polar roles, and the continuity between our friends doesn't have the historical dimension of regeneration or recreation. It is temporally "horizontal" rather than "vertical." Between friends, we don't identify with both and feel ourselves responsible for their identifying with one another.

Even the ideal parent-adult child relationship can't be a complete friendship. Inequality in autonomy (within the relationship) and lack of relational autonomy (independence from one another) keep parents and children from a fully realized friendship. However, at its best, the parent-adult child relationship contains valuable qualities which are missing from even ideal friendships. The identification, love, stability, and aesthetic closure enrich the parent-adult child relationship in unique ways. We ought not, therefore, lament the fact that friendship doesn't quite capture what the parent-adult child relationship should aspire to. For even as it is in some respects less than complete friendship, so does it also offer what friendship cannot.

CHAPTER FIVE

Privacy, Autonomy, and Self-Concept

In our age of electronic surveillance, centralized data banks, and computerized solicitation, the topic of privacy is eliciting a good deal of attention. But what is the value of privacy, of freedom from surveillance or information-gathering? The view I shall argue for here is that privacy is a necessary condition for something of basic value—the development of an automonous self.

In the first place, privacy is needed for the development of our faculties whose exercise helps constitute autonomy. Secondly, automony requires a conception of self for which privacy is indispensible. In particular, a concept of self as empowered to determine one's life is requisite to thinking and acting automonously. And privacy is needed for such a self-concept to develop. Before articulating and defending this view of the connection between privacy and autonomy, we should first look at what privacy is as well as other possible values it may have.

Privacy and Its Value

Although the scope of this chapter does not permit wading through the host of subtleties and qualifications that define different senses of privacy, some rough and ready notion needs to be offered, if only to avoid certain confusions and objections.

Privacy includes some control over some information about oneself. I purposely leave both the degree of control and range of information unspecified, and for two reasons. It suits our present inquiry, and greater specification of degree of control and range of information is quite difficult to make out. Surely privacy does not require absolute control over all the things that can be construed as "about" the self.

The attempt to limit privacy to control over certain items runs aground on the fact that loss of control over almost any particular item is sometimes related to privacy, sometimes not. Whether someone knows our religion, to whom we're married, or our bank balance, may or may not be a private matter, depending on the context and our relationship to that person. What is private in relation to my spouse is very different from what is private in relation to an employer or mere acquaintance.

His attempt to state precisely what "about the self" is private, for example, prevents Stanley I. Benn from providing a non-question-begging defense of a right to privacy on the basis of respect for persons. He tries to limit the restrictions on others' freedom to observe or gather information about us.

> It must be something about my own person that is in question, otherwise the principle would be so wide that a mere wish of mine would be a prima facie reason for everyone to refrain from observing and reporting on anything at all.[1]

Benn begs the question of what makes something private by referring to what amounts to an allegedly "private" sphere—one's "own person" or "self."

Because Benn cannot provide independent grounds for showing that an individual has a right not to have his "own self" appropriated, he reformulates rather than grounds the right to privacy. Jeffrey Reiman convincingly convicts Benn of a *petitio principii*. Reiman argues that Benn's attempt to limit the area of control over which the individual has the right to exclude others requires this additional claim for support: "The closer something is to my identity, the worse it is for others to tamper with it. But this is after all just an abstract version of the right to privacy itself."[2] Benn's difficulty in defending a right to privacy grows out of his attempt to pin down the definition of the concept.

This is probably the best place to acknowledge still another "indefiniteness" in the concept of privacy: the variability of the concept's application in different societies. While the meaning or import of privacy may be fairly constant across cultures, what counts as privacy or its violation clearly varies considerably. For example, we experience inroads in our "personal space" as a violation of privacy. But this space is defined differently in different cultures. "An American in the Middle East or Latin America is likely to feel crowded and hemmed in—people come too close, lay their hands on him, and crowd against his body."[3] Cultural relativity in the application of the concept of privacy, of course, doesn't show that what privacy is changes.

Beyond some control over some information about us, privacy also seems to involve control over who can experience or "sense" us. Sometimes control over who can experience or sense us amounts simply to control over information about us, but not always. When experience of us conveys no new information, for example, then loss of control over who experiences us is a distinct matter, demanding its own place in the understanding of privacy. Richard B. Parker persuasively argues that some losses of control over who can perceive us are not reducible to loss of control over information about us and that such losses constitute loss of privacy. He gives this helpful example:

> Consider also the case of a woman's lover who, just after he has left her side, peers in through the window in order to see her once more in the nude. She has suffered a loss of privacy, yet it seems inaccurate to describe her loss of privacy as a loss of control of information about herself. Her lover knows that her body has not changed, that she has not put on her clothes. Yet the essence of her loss of privacy is not a loss of control over information . . . It is a loss of control over who, at that moment, can see her body.[4]

What our serviceable characterization of privacy comes to, then, is this: Privacy includes some control over some information about us and who can experience us.

What of the value of this privacy? It is either extrinsically or intrinsically good. The view I argue for in this chapter is that privacy is extrinsically valuable, good in relation to something distinct from itself. However, this doesn't make privacy merely contingently good. For although not good in itself, it is necessary for another good—autonomy. I don't wish to deny the other extrinsic values of privacy, values which are contingent. Thus, privacy certainly does secure us from misuse or abuse of information about us. And privacy enables us to engage in activities which we might be too inhibited to engage in if we thought others could observe us. This is all well and good, but I think that the value of privacy goes beyond such contingencies. It is worth having even if such threats or inhibitions are absent. This is why it is important to secure the value of privacy more firmly.

At the other extreme are attempts to provide the strongest of grounds for the value of privacy: that it is intrinsically good. The problem with this view is that it is terribly difficult to articulate what is good about privacy without connecting it to other, more basic goods (such as autonomy or peace of mind). Most attempts to explain why privacy is good in itself quickly become circular. Thus, Thomas Scanlon claims that various privacy rights, "Have a common foundation in the special interests that we have in being able to be free from certain kinds of intrusion."[5]

While this at first appears helpful and convincing, the sort of scrutiny Reiman brings to bear reveals that Scanlon's "special interests" simply define privacy. The right to privacy simply is the right "to be free from certain kinds of intrusions." As Reiman points out,

> Scanlon's position is equivalent to holding that the common foundation of our right to privacy lies in our 'privatistic interests.' . . . What Scanlon has not told us is why we have a special interest in privacy, that is, a special interest in being free from certain kinds of intrusions.[6]

And this, of course, is to show the value of privacy or privatistic interests in light of some other good, and so to give up on its intrinsic value.

The view I am proposing, then, sees privacy as more than merely contingently good, but not quite valuable in itself. As necessary for something of basic value, privacy is not just contingently good. But, since privacy derives its value from its relation to this other good thing, autonomy, privacy is not good in itself.

Since the view offered here involves related causal claims, its ultimate vindication will require empirical support.[7] I will, in fact, cite some evidence as well as professional conjecture to buttress my claims; however, the evidence is far from conclusive. Most studies are of situations which include variables besides privacy (so, the effects on autonomy could be "overdetermined") and we lack repeated studies for sufficiently similar conditions. A satisfactory rejection of my view, however, would require more than empirical counter-examples (such as people growing up with little privacy but lots of autonomy). What would also be needed is an alternative account of how autonomy does indeed develop in these un-private circumstances. This would involve a rival moral psychology with perhaps its own philosophical analysis of self-concept.[8]

Developing the Faculties

What we must now examine is the way that privacy is essential to the development and maintenance of an autonomous self. Central in this enterprise will be a detailed account of the role of privacy in the formation of a particular sort of self-concept. But first we need to look at a more straightforward contribution privacy makes to autonomy: the way it enables the development of certain faculties.

Lack of privacy, quite simply, is likely to inhibit us from doing and saying many things which we would otherwise do and say. For a variety of reasons we refrain from some behavior because we don't wish others to know about it. Of course, this isn't all bad; such inhibition can have salutary consequences as well as those that debilitate. Now the immediate effect of this inhibition on autonomy is to limit our options. We don't exercise our autonomy as fully or widely as we would if we had privacy.

> If we thought that our every word and deed were public, fear of disapproval or more tangible retaliation might keep us from doing or saying things which we would do or say if we could be sure of keeping them to ourselves or within a circle of those who we know approve or tolerate our tastes.[9]

But this inhibition is likely to have more far-reaching, indirect consequences on our autonomy. It is likely to stifle the development of the faculties which govern what we say and do. For by inhibiting the speech and action in the first place, lack of privacy also curtails the development of the faculties responsible for what we say and do. Our faculties of thought, feeling, imagining, and choosing are stifled when denied expression and efficacy in behavior. Privacy provides an area of choice in what we say and do that would otherwise be lacking. It is by choosing freely that our deliberative repertoire itself expands and deepens.

Isaiah Berlin argues that we cannot develop these faculties without a minimum zone of inviolable freedom.

> If it [this zone] is overstepped, the individual will find himself in an area too narrow for even that minimum development of his natural faculties which alone makes it possible to pursue, and even to conceive, the various ends which men hold good or right or sacred.[10]

Knowing that others will not interfere with us enables us to develop in ways necessary to pursue and attain our ends. But perhaps even more profoundly, as Berlin notes, we need privacy in order to conceive of the needs we wish to pursue.

Now in one sense this is probably false. We don't need privacy to conceive of ends which are socially offered or dictated. It's quite easy to conceive of what others tell and show us they are interested in or pressure us to have an interest in. What we do need privacy for is the development of the powers needed to conceive our own ends, to project our own scenarios and deliberate about them. We also need privacy to develop our ability to reflect on how our choices have turned out—what went right or wrong and why.

In particular, we need privacy to develop that faculty which is pivotal to the blooming of autonomy—the imagination. As we have seen in earlier chapters, autonomy includes the ability to make plans and decide for oneself what to do. To "make plans" and decide for oneself necessarily involve the individual in projecting herself into a variety of possible futures. This projecting, essential to the having of projects, involves seeing possibilities not yet real. We must be able to imagine changeable futures in order to direct ourselves toward ends that our truly our own. The richer our imaginations, the wider the range and the fuller the detail of these possible futures. We are less bound to what has already been actualized, much of which is the result of circumstances over which we have not exercised autonomy. The stronger our imaginations, the more the needs and projects which we eventually undertake are our own. And this also goes for imagining the means toward their realization, a subject which we will not pursue here.

Mary Mothersill insightfully locates the role of the imagination in the autonomous life.

> Now the imagination is above all else that in virtue of which we can be independent. Whatever our situation we can think as we please, interpret as we please, and feel as we are led by our own interpretations . . . the education of the imagination is to be valued because it is the only possible education for freedom.[11]

While this last sentence probably overstates the case a bit, Mothersill has certainly put her finger on the imagination's liberating function.

Our imaginative powers need to be cultivated, educated. Regardless of "how much" imagination we have been endowed with, its potential needs to be developed. The question of what is needed to cultivate the imagination is obviously too big for us to take up here, but the importance of privacy in its cultivation (and, hence, the expansion of autonomy) is germane. Again, Mothersill is illuminating:

> I do not believe that it is possible to educate the imagination without ensuring for every pupil a certain degree of solitude . . . since imagination is not merely perceptual but also emotional and interpretational, its exercise takes time, and a degree of contemplation. I believe that perpetual society destroys the imaginative faculty, and that children who fear solitude and are bored immediately they are alone are becoming deprived in this very respect.[12]

What we can conclude, then, is this. Autonomy requires the development of various human faculties. Some of these faculties will be blunted simply from the inhibitory effects of lack of privacy. Inhibition from saying and doing certain things limits the growth of the faculties employed in such sayings and doings. Further, the faculties can be stifled through lack of opportunity to conceive and contemplate ends and projects. In particular, developing the imagination, central in projecting ourselves into possible futures, requires freedom from interference and surveillance. This account of the importance of privacy to the development of human faculties will be taken up in the next section when we analyze second-order autonomy and the self-conscious shaping of the self.

Autonomy and Self-Concept

We come now to the central claim of this chapter. Privacy is needed for the formation of the sort of self-concept essential to autonomous living. While there is a good deal more to autonomy (as we have seen in Chapter I), it includes a concept of oneself as a purposeful, self-determining, responsible agent. Autonomy includes awareness of oneself as determining both particular courses of action as well as an overall life-plan. This is because autonomy entails the ability and disposition to make plans and decide for oneself what to do. We envision various scenarios for our future, shaped around our desires which are potentially at odds with the desires and interests of others.

Such planning and deciding require a concept of self as empowered to determine our life according to our own purposes and lights. Unless the individual conceives of himself as in control of his life, as self-determining, he cannot function autonomously. We might call this an "autonomous self-concept." Using it to characterize autonomy is not circular since we have an independent notion of "autonomous self-concept:" conceivng of oneself as a purposeful, self-determining, responsible agent. In addition, autonomy involves a good deal more than this self-concept.

A. Bodily Identification

An autonomous self-concept requires identifying with a particular body whose thoughts, purposes, and actions are subject to one's control. We conceive of ourselves as having choice in what happens to us by acting, in particular, by exercising choice over something that others do not exercise choice over. The self-reflexive nature of autonomy in the development of our capacities of choice and control is captured in the observation that, "Autonomy encompasses . . . the awareness of volition as a means of controlling the boundary between self and other."[13] Perhaps the most evident boundary is that provided by our bodies.

Our bodies are a basic locus of agency, an early site of self-definition. R.S. Peters nicely expands upon this notion.

> People only begin to think of themselves as persons, centers of valuation, decision, and choice, in so far as the fact that consciousness is individuated into distinct centers, linked with distinct physical bodies and with distinctive points of view, is taken to be a matter of importance in a society. And they will only really develop as persons in so far as they learn to think of themselves as such.[14]

Peters makes two important observations which should here be distinguished. First, bodily identification and control don't occur in isolation. We see ourselves as in control of this body in conjunction with thoughts, desires, action-plans, and bodily movement itself. We learn to identify with our bodies in the course of doing things. Our own point of view consists of valuations, affect, and decisions, realized (in part) through control of our bodies. Our psychology is embodied, and our bodies are psychologically informed. Without control of our bodies and awareness of this control, it is doubtful that we would experience ourselves as psychological centers of determination. Secondly, to arrive at bodily identification and control certain social relations are necessary.

We need social practices and institutions to assign importance to individual points of view. Privacy is one of the ways in which society fosters what Peters calls the "assertive point of view." It is not enough simply to be free from others' interference; autonomy requires awareness of control over one's relation to others, including their access to us. An individual who was free from interference by others but did not realize it, for example, would hardly be autonomous. Her choices and actions would still be determined from without, by her pereption of the desires and purposes of others. No matter how free from external restraint, an individual is not in control of her life, is not self-determining, unless she conceives of herself as such. Which is to say that autonomy requires an autonomous self-concept. Control over our bodies, thoughts, and actions, is conveyed, therefore, through our interaction with others.

Developing a conception of self as autonomous through the exercise of choice in ends and their pursuit requires that others affirm the social boundaries of this self. They must grant the individual control over her physical movements and information about herself. They must also permit the individual to have some say in who can experience her and when. We "naturally" come to think of particular purposes or ends as our own only because we experience others as permitting us to pursue them without interference. In this way, a concept of self develops which includes the ends the individual has chosen and can pursue physically through her own choice. Autonomy, therefore, is a social product, the result of various social practices which encourage self-determination, including those forming the institution of privacy.

B. First-Order Autonomy

Privacy contributes to the formation and flourishing of autonomous people by providing them with control over whether or not their physical and psychological existence becomes part of another's experience. Just this sort of control over others' access to us is necessary for us to think of ourselves as self-determining. In particular, to see ourselves as able to think our own thoughts, capable of independent choice, and empowered to act so as to get what we want. The autonomy of this self-concept is first-order; it is concerned with particular thoughts and desires, concrete choices and plans of action. To conceive of oneself as autonomous in this first-order sense is to conceive of oneself as directly affecting his world, bringing it into line with his interests and purposes (rather than determining the very nature of those interests and purposes).

Evidence for this view that privacy promotes autonomy by fostering an autonomous self-concept is found in studies of both identity development and deterioration. Psychologists such as Jean Piaget and Victor Tausk attest to the child's growing sense of self as attendant upon an understanding of her control over information about herself. Experiencing privacy, secrecy, even lying, conveys to the child that many things remain hidden unless she chooses to reveal them. As she understands herself as determining whether and to what degree others have access to her, the child develops an autonomous self-concept. She sees herself as having some power to determine what happens to her. She can exercise the control over particular objects and people characteristic of first-order autonomy.[15]

Even more dramatically, studies of adults who are systematically, chronically denied privacy find deterioration in their autonomy. The total loss of privacy characteristic of Orwell's totalitarian society is found today in "total institutions," such as prisons. As Erving Goffman observes in *Asylums*:

> On the outside, the individual can hold objects of self-feeling—such as his body, his immediate actions, his thoughts, and some of his possessions—clear of contact with alien and contaminating things. But in total institutions these *territories* of the *self* are *violated* . . .[16]

As a result, the individual's self-concept shrinks to fit his powerless condition and his autonomy is diminished.

A similar story unfolds in nursing homes, hospitals, military establishments, and religious orders. To the extent that they are deprived of privacy, people tend to lose the sense of themselves as origins of thought, purpose, and action. For example, the range of choices exercised by patients in hospital psychiatric wards was found to vary inversely with the size of the room and number of beds. In smaller rooms patients exercised greater freedom of choice, engaging in a wide range of behaviors; while in larger ones, isolated, passive behavior prevailed. The diminished exercise of choice, accompanied by increased passivity, bespeaks erosion of autonomy.[17]

In the 1950's, in a large, overcrowded ward of Saint Elizabeth's Hospital in Washington, spatial limitations on autonomy led to enuresis.

> At the bottom of the [hierarchical] ladder, the omega had the use of nothing more than the bench on which he slept . . . As soon as they were given access to a decent amount of space, 50 percent of these patients ceased to be incontinent.[18]

As acknowledged earlier, studies such as these provide less than conclusive empirical support for my claim. The conditions being studied involve serious losses besides privacy; inmates typically are isolated from the outside world, are restricted in dress and movement, and lose control over what is done to them. Can we even conclude that privacy loss is a contributing causal factor? Perhaps it is merely a causally inefficacious correlate. This is certainly possible, but without further evidence to support it, such conjecture must remain such. These kinds of studies would seem to lend presumptive support to the view presented here, especially in light of the child development research which points in the same direction.

C. *Second-Order Autonomy*

So far we have explained how privacy is needed for what might be considered a "basic" autonomous self-concept to develop and endure. This is privacy's contribution to our first-order autonomy—the way speaking to a child contributes to a first-order language mastery. But there is a further way in which privacy fosters the kind of self-concept essential to autonomy. Privacy enables self-knowledge, self-criticism, and self-evaluation. This sort of *control* over self-concept and self is a second-order autonomy. It is analogous to the second-order mastery of language enjoyed when the individual acquires the ability to self-consciously compose, aware of alternatives in expression and style. How exactly is privacy necessary to the second-order autonomy which devolves upon a self-examined self-concept?

Hyman Gross makes the following suggestion:

> Respect for privacy is required to safeguard our changes of mood and mind, and to promote growth of the person through self-discovery and criticism. We want to run the risk of making fools of ourselves and be free to call ourselves fools, yet not be fools in the settled opinion of the world, convicted out of our own mouths.[19]

We need privacy to rehearse our thinking and behavior, to try out options without running "real life" risks. Privacy secures, even prompts, the critical examination of the beliefs, desires, and attitudes that determine our first-order ends.

If the "growth" that Gross speaks of is closely connected with autonomy, then his observation about privacy's role in self-discovery and self-criticism eventually bears also on autonomy. The idea here is that a person who has grown through self-discovery and self-criticism enjoys greater autonomy than one who does not. Why so? Because someone, say, who knows his weaknesses and his limits is in a better position to determine what will happen to him than someone who lacks this sort of self-knowledge. Choices have a way of building on one another, accumulating in their effects. Knowing one's limits enables an individual to choose so as to be able to *continue* to exert maximal control over his life in the future. His choices can further future choosings rather than frustrate or merely idle alongside them. A person living this way has greater autonomy than one who does not. This can be seen as an extension of the way the development of our basic faculties, discussed earlier, makes possible the more basic level of autonomy. But I think the connection between self-criticism and autonomy goes even deeper.

The notion that the self-critical, self-knowledgeable person is more automonous than another is deepened when we realize that autonomy can be exercised over the self as such. One who has greater control over who and what she is is thereby more autonomous. Charles Taylor describes a basic level at which self-criticism and revision may operate.

> Beyond the *de facto* characterization of the subject by his goals, desires, and purposes, a person is a subject who can pose the *de jure* question: is this the kind of being I ought to be, or really want to be?[20]

One who evaluates her very self—her deepest convictions about what a good or noble life consists in—exercises more autonomy over her life than someone who does not. Such a person engages in a self-reflection which is an exercise of autonomy over self-concept and thence selfhood. "It is a reflection about the self, its most fundamental issues,"[21] and involves asking, "Have I really understood what is essential to my identity? Have I truly determined what I sense to be the highest mode of life?"[22] One who does not ask these fundamental questions about herself determines less of her life than one who does. Rather, her most deeply held convictions remain inchoate, haphazardly formed in the hurly-burly of daily life and its unperceived influences.

The most complete autonomy involves integrating the disparate interests and projects that we have. Bringing them together in a coherent pattern, itself an exercise in autonomy, gives us greater control over each, at least in avoiding endeavors which cancel each other's ends out. And, at best, in undertaking projects which further one another.

There may also be greater autonomy in having an integrated personality, as Adina Schwartz suggests.

> Becoming autonomous is not a matter of coming to exercise intelligence and initiative in a number of separate areas of one's life. Rather, it is a process of integrating one's personality: of coming to see all one's pursuits as subject to one's activity of planning and to view all one's experiences as providing a basis for evaluating and adjusting one's beliefs, methods, and aims.[23]

Her idea seems to be that the integrated personality has a view of the whole: the whole of experience and how it self-consciously figures in shaping one's beliefs and behavior. Drawing on one's life as a whole in deciding what to do and why to do it gives one greater autonomy. Life as a whole, then, is within the control only of the integrated personality, one who conceives life in this way.

This sort of self-definition, what Benn calls "self-creation," requires privacy. Privacy provides us with a sheltered context for deciding how to act and be in the world. Not only deciding, but rehearsing and preparing to change to fit the idea of self which has been developed through the auspices of our second-order autonomy. Control over information about oneself, "Must be understood as a basic part of the right to shape the 'self' that one presents to the world, and on the basis of which the world in turn shapes one's existence."[24] In this passage, Laurence Tribe calls our attention to the dialectical nature of this self-creation.

The self that privacy enables us to mold is, in turn, influenced by the public world. That public world will react differently, of course, depending on the nature of the self we present to it. Hence, the double significance of the privacy. It enables the psychological space for self-creation. But this itself has a further impact on self-formation, since the self which we present will elicit different responses from the public world, which responses in turn further shape our self.

We shall see in the next chapter how the public and private are dialectically related in general, even to the point of reciprocally determining one another. Here we have emphasized how the private makes possible a certain public persona. There the emphasis will be more on how the public can create room for privacy.

Sometimes the self we choose to develop will be in conflict with social norms and expectations. We will decide to follow a plan of life as well as self that will meet with objections from others. To formulate such a conception, much less to begin to try to realize it, requires some protection from this potential conflict.

> In privacy we can develop, over time, a firmer, better constructed, and more integrated position in opposition to the dominant social pressures. And this is surely one of its central contributions to the development of individuality, of distinct and independent selves.[25]

In order to develop a self potentially at odds with the world, we need distance from that world. We need to escape from the image others have of us or which they wish to see us fulfill. Barry Schwartz points out how the identity imposed on us by others is bound up with role expectations, and how privacy helps negate this imposition of identity. "The very act of placing a barrier between oneself and others is self-defining, for withdrawal entails a separation from a role, and tacitly, from an identity imposed upon oneself by others via that role."[26] Privacy, then, gives us the freedom from the pressure to fulfill a social identity needed to create, as autonomously as possible, the self we truly wish to be.

Privacy provides a necessary context for the self-scrutiny, self-evaluation, and self-creation, which constitute second-order autonomy. By insuring against others as intrusion, threat, and distraction, privacy enables us to determine for ourselves our self-concept and the self which depends upon it. Without this second-order autonomy, moreover, there is a diminution of first-order autonomy insofar as one's daily choices and control flow from this self-conception. After all, the particular decisions and actions which we engage in tend to vary with the way we more generally define and shape our selves. To the extent that our self-concept is determined from without, to that extent our first-order decisions are also derivative.

Moral Dimensions of Self-Concept

Through its moral impact on our self-concept privacy further contributes to autonomy. Not only does privacy enable an autonomous self-concept, but it is also needed to morally inform that concept in certain ways. In particular, privacy is needed to promote a concept of the self as trustworthy: worthy of acting autonomously, of making independent choices and controlling one's life.

Privacy as freedom from surveillance[27] gives the individual room to make mistakes or do wrong. By allowing the individual to go out of sight or earshot, others threat him as trustworthy.[28] He conceives himself as absent-to-others and knows that this is permitted by them. The particular self that is generated by this social practice is not simply a removable entity, able to take itself away from others. It is also an entity *worthy* of being *left* alone. Conceiving of oneself as possessing this kind of worth is a sort of moral extension of the autonomous self-concept.

> A particular kind of privacy is necessary when the learning of responsibility is at stake. Not only must there be opportunities for activity which may result in increasingly serious mistakes, there must be a degree of tolerance for idiosyncratic forms of behavior quite at variance with the norms of the older generation.[29]

By providing opportunity for failure, wrong-doing, or deviance, society indicates confidence in the individual's exercise of autonomy—faith in the overall quality of purpose, choice, and action.

To develop this sense of trustworthiness, of course, the individual must justify the faith of others by acting responsibly. He must respond dependably to this independence, making careful if not always correct decisions. Being responsible in this "moral achievement" sense (and not simply causal or morally accountable sense) is, however, tied to correct decision-making. It implies that the individual generally has what it takes to make good decisions. Morally responsible people deliberate intelligently and usually make sound choices.

Believing ourselves worthy of the trust of others is necessary, moreover, for us to learn to trust ourselves. We cannot come to count on ourselves, to have confidence in the quality of our choices and actions without believing ourselves worthy of the trust of others. More to the point, trusting in ourselves equips us psychologically to take the risks inherent in autonomous action. Making independent decisions and taking responsibility for them leave us vulnerable to error and subsequent criticism. Fear of failure or mistake in particular choices, however, can be offset by a general sense of trustworthiness. This is especially true because a sense of worthiness of trust fuels an individual's overall estimation of self-worth. While there can be other grounds for self-worth, such as technical accomplishment, trustworthiness is an especially moral ground, constitutive of autonomy. Armed with the sense of self-worth that turns upon belief in one's own trustworthiness, an individual has a kind of moral confidence in his choice-making abilities. Autonomous action comes "naturally" to those with a conviction in their own moral self-worth.

Encouraging an individual to believe that she is worthy of trust because capable of responsibly exercising her autonomy may be pivotal to protecting her autonomy. If an individual relies on others to protect her autonomy she is more likely to lose it than if she asserts herself and is on the alert for incursions in her autonomy. The individual who feels worthy of being trusted to behave responsibly has both the disposition and justification for fending off inroads into her autonomy. So, if we are concerned to maximize autonomy in general, concerned lest people lose what autonomy they have (or fail to develop what they can), then strengthening their sense of trustworthiness and self-worth is a likely cornerstone.

Privacy contributes to self-respect and self-esteem in a fairly straightforward way by giving people a chance to recover from social interaction that tears them down. Sociologist Alan Bates observes that people need privacy for restoring self-esteem after "bruising" social contact, and for rationalizing disapproved conduct and inclinations.[30] Free of the society or censure of others, the individual is able to interpret her behavior in such ways as renew her sense of worth. I should add that this often takes place with intimates, in the shared moments privacy makes possible.

Being granted privacy enhances self-worth because it is a way of treating someone with respect. As Stanley Benn has argued,

> Respect for someone as a person, as a chooser, implie[s] respect for him as one engaged on a kind of self-creative enterprise, which could be disrupted, distorted, or frustrated even by so limited an intrusion as watching.[31]

To respect someone as a chooser (as autonomous) is to grant him freedom from interference or limitation in the form of privacy.

If Benn is correct, then to deprive someone of privacy is more than merely constraining or inhibiting. It is also degrading; the individual feels the intrusion as lack of respect. Not necessarily that he isn't capable of choosing correctly, hence, lack of trustworthiness. But rather that his projects and feelings, including feelings of self-worth, aren't important or valuable enough to check the other's intruding impulses. When we violate someone's privacy we don't respect him, "as engaged on an enterprise worthy of consideration."[32] According to Benn, we don't acknowledge the importance to the individual of his activity and therefore the importance or value of the individual himself.

When we treat people with disrespect by failing to grant them privacy we thereby *convey* this lack of respect to them. If this happens often enough or meaningfully enough (say, at the hands of those who are highly esteemed), then the individual whose privacy is violated is likely to suffer loss of self-respect. His self-concept will lack an important constituent, a constituent that in turn supports autonomous behavior.

Our "enterprise" of self-creation is usually tied to productive work, to the creation of things or ideas. We create ourselves, and our self-concept, by objectifying ourselves in our creations. Privacy provides a place to work on projects free of others' judgments. It gives us control not only over who sees the products of our labor, but when they do, as well. "The dignity of the human being requires that he be judged only on the basis of those products he decides to make public . . ."[33] Therefore, we show respect for someone by allowing him to decide when to present himself as objectified in his work. Privacy is integral to doing this.

Although detailed analysis of public institutions is not within the scope of this book, the following example convincingly illustrates how deprivation of privacy is likely to diminish people's self-respect and also underscores the way physical arrangements can promote or restrict privacy.

> There is no physical freedom whatsoever at Milgrim [High School]. . . No time at which, or place in which, a student may simply go about his business. Privacy is strictly forbidden. Except during class breaks, the toilets are kept locked, so that a student must not only obtain a pass but find the custodian and induce him to unlock the facility.[34]

Withholding opportunities for people, especially students struggling with self-definition and self-worth, to opt for privacy conveys a degrading message. Either they cannot be trusted to be left alone or their wishes and needs are not to be regarded seriously. This devaluing is likely to reduce the individuals' sense of trustworthiness or self-respect, or both. It is clearly a force antagonistic to the creation and maintenance of the positive self-concept from which autonomous action naturally flows.

Considerations of autonomy also distinguish privacy from isolation. Isolating an individual does not promote a sense of trustworthiness because isolation is mere deprivation of social contact over which the individual has no control. In such practices as banishment or shunning, for example, the individual is not himself choosing whether or not to interact. Rather, others choose circumstances which limit or remove the individual's choice. When someone enjoys privacy, however, he has choice and control over interaction or disclosure of information about himself. It is precisely the exercise of autonomy, central to genuine privacy, that is missing in isolation. We elect solitude, but suffer isolation.

Privacy is a trusting way others treat us, resulting in a conception of ourselves as worth being trusted. In contrast, monitoring behavior or collecting data on us projects a disvaluing of the self in question. Depending on the individual and the extent of privacy loss, the individual's sense of trustworthiness is threatened. Loss of privacy tends either to obstruct the formation of a sense of trustworthiness or erode one already formed.

In the previous section, however, it was argued that lack of privacy threatened something more basic than either a sense of trustworthiness or self-worth. There it was argued that privacy is necessary to maintain an autonomous self-concept and the autonomous self which depends on it. If that is correct, then continued surveillance should eventually go beyond diminution in self-worth and undermine autonomy itself. This suggests that with increasing loss of privacy the individual should suffer a corresponding loss— on a continuum from a sense of trustworthiness or self-worth to autonomy. It should be noted that positing such proportional loss implies no causal link between loss of a sense of self-worth and diminished autonomy. It may be that some level of self-worth is needed for autonomous functioning (for the reason cited above). But decrease in self-worth need not be causally connected to erosion of autonomy to precede it on a continuum which corresponds to loss of privacy.

Social Self-Concept—Intimacy

Privacy also has a social bearing on self-concept and autonomy because of its importance to intimacy. Some philosophers go so far as to locate the value of privacy exclusively in its role as a necessary condition for intimacy and friendship.[35] Charles Fried, for instance, argues that privacy enables the individual to withhold information about himself from some and bestow it on others. On this analysis, privacy makes personal information a scarce commodity, unavailable to most people, and thereby a thing of value.[36]

When we share information about ourselves with someone, therefore, we share something made valuable because made scarce or special by privacy. This valuable commodity is the stuff of intimacy, making for a special relationship. On the other hand, if we lacked privacy, the personal information would not be exclusive and we would consequently lack the valuable commodity whose sharing makes for intimacy. On this view, then, privacy is necessary to make information about ourselves valuable, and such valuable information is necessary for intimacy and friendship.[37]

But this does not seem quite right. Even if possession of information is necesary for intimacy and friendship, it is surely not sufficient. Rather, as Jeffrey Reiman points out, a context of caring makes information valuable.[38] Caring about those to whom we disclose personal information makes that information relevant to intimacy. Reiman, however, goes further, arguing that privacy is not even necessary to intimacy or friendship. If people other than friends possess information about us, perhaps through loss of privacy, our capacity for intimacy is not thereby diminished; our "moral capital" is in no way depleted. This is because the information about us is not used up by those "strangers," and we can still share it, as well as "intense experiences," with those about whom we care.

While I tend to agree with Reiman's general criticism of Fried's "commodity" view of the importance of privacy, I think it overlooks an important bearing privacy does have on intimacy. In particular, by providing control over information about and access to ourselves, privacy enables us to define ourselves socially in terms of intimate relationships. Our self-concept does, indeed, depend upon who our intimates are, in part because our *self* does. By ignoring the role of privacy in the forming of both a social self and self-concept, Reiman misses the way loss of privacy poses a particular threat to autonomy.

Belief that someone we care about returns that affection and concern is usually the basis for *voluntarily* sharing information about ourselves. It is this voluntary, autonomous character of the means by which others come into possession of personal information that really links intimacy with privacy. Privacy insures the autonomous nature of the transmission of this personal information. This intimacy enables an "opening" to others, an opening which shapes who we are.

> Company *a deux* is not merely pleasant—it is a precondition for that part of identity development that [Erik H.] Erikson describes as 'losing and finding oneself in another.' We become what we are not only by establishing boundaries around ourselves but also by a periodic opening of these boundaries to nourishment, learning, and to intimacy.[39]

Privacy allows us to choose who we open ourselves up to, as well as when and how we do it. We autonomously choose to be shaped by *this* person and *this* relationship. Even though we don't fully control the relationship and how we are changed as a result of it, we have still acted autonomously in forming the relationship and disclosing ourselves in it.

Because voluntarily offered information fosters intimacy, when it is taken without our permission, the appearance of intimacy may be created. This appearance, even presumption of intimacy subtly calls our autonomy into question by threatening our self-conception. How exactly does it do this?

The concept we have of ourselves includes who our intimates are. It also includes our control (or lack of control) in determining who they are. Control over both our intimate relationships and their particular content define us. We not only identify ourselves as Jones' friend but also as someone who determines whether Jones is her friend. We do the latter, in part, by controlling personal information. When the appearance of intimacy is created through loss of privacy, and the ensuing loss of control over who can experience or know about us, our self-concept is threatened. By blurring the distinction between intimate and stranger, the pseudo-intimacy seems to force a "false" entry into our self-concept. It impinges on the content of our self-conception, if only in the realm of appearances, and thereby threatens our sense of control over it. We feel as if we had no choice concerning who our friends really are, as if anyone by his choice could make himself our intimate.

This sense of threat is sometimes felt when a mere acquaintance claps us on the shoulder, grins, and alludes to a camaraderie not really there. We feel a presumption on his part and, correlatively, an invasion of our autonomy by this creation of pseudo-intimacy. It is like someone stealing a kiss from us. The stolen kiss does not cheapen the value of our kisses (as Fried's commodity view would have it) nor make their autonomous giving impossible. Rather, it usurps our control over who receives these expressions of affection. Because both the control over and content of our self-conception are tampered with, we feel violated. The autonomy to determine our social self-concept is called into question.

We ought, then, to draw a weaker conclusion than Fried wishes to. Privacy and control over information about ourselves may not be strictly necessary to forming intimate relationships. However, it is crucial to the strength of our autonomous self-conception because of its bearing on intimacy. Loss of privacy can weaken the concept of ourselves as autonomous by threatening our sense of control over who our intimates are.

Believed vs. Actual Privacy

The account of the value of privacy offered above is fairly broad, based on the formation and preservation of an autonomous self and expanding to include moral and social dimensions of self-concept. But it has one apparently awkward consequence. Strictly speaking, it does not reveal the value of actual privacy so much as belief in its existence. Under undetected surveillence, believing herself "in private", an individual could well develop autonomously (with a high degree of self-worth, unthreatened by presumptions or appearances of intimacy). We think of ourselves as self-determing because we believe that we control a body, thoughts, and actions others do not. We identify ourselves with our purposes, our ability to act responsibly, and the intimate relationships we have established. These can all occur even if we are under continuous surveillance, so long as we are unaware of it and think we enjoy a fair measure of privacy.

This would seem especially damaging for my position since covert spying may be more of an infringement on our autonomy by deceiving us about our actual status. At least when we know that we lack privacy we can inhibit ourselves and to some extent prevent others from acquiring information about us. So, if perfectly executed covert spying is compatible with the value claimed for privacy above, that would seem unfortunate indeed.

The perspective of Orwell's *1984*, however, suggests a practical way out of this difficulty. When surveillance is institutionalized by the state, the practical impossibility of keeping it hidden is incompatible with belief in privacy. The subsequent deterioration in autonomy would then follow. It is virtually impossible that the instruments for invading the privacy of a whole society themselves be kept private. They must become public, as in *1984*. My account of the value of privacy, then, provides a basis for the social institution of privacy rather than privacy per se. The necessity of privacy for the development and maintenance of an autonomous self-concept, as well as certain moral and social features of it, grounds the *public policy* of privacy, arguing against a totalitarian state.

For those who are uncomfortable with a conclusion which does not establish the absolute need for or value of actual privacy, consider the following possibility. Imagine a state which manipulated its people into believing that they were under constant surveillance when in fact they were not! In order to inhibit the people and prevent disorderly or individualized behavior, the authorities convince the people that they have no privacy—perhaps through dummy television cameras, spot monitoring, and the like. The fact that the people indeed do enjoy privacy is of little account. They would think and act as though completely exposed. In fact, from the standpoint of developing and maintaining autonomy they would be much worse off than their counterparts in the mirror-society in which privacy is believed but not real.

CHAPTER SIX

Building Autonomous Places

Even if we assume that parents and early environment conspire to make us relatively autonomous, we need a lived context that is going to facilitate the development and exercise of autonomy. Autonomy, like a skill, requires ongoing encouragement. On the other hand, for those who are only marginally autonomous, the context in which they live is crucial to whether their autonomy remains minimal or reaches higher levels. The aspect of this "context" which I will now examine is the built environment, "architecture," for short. It includes interior design, land and street organization, as well as the more obvious "buildings" that define our lived space.

In many ways this is the opposite side of the privacy which we just discussed. Just as autonomy depends on a sense of private "space" (both literal and figurative), so too does it depend on the contours of public space. A great deal of the architecture with which we interact is "public." It is unavoidable and pervasive; anyone, if not everyone, in a given community or population will be affected by much of the architecture. Even so-called "private" dwellings have an impact on neighbors and passersby.

I will talk about the "private" spaces created by architecture; however, the emphasis will be on the public—areas that are open and available to anyone. The public character of such architecture makes it a serious causal force in influencing the development and exercise of autonomy. Because architecture is pervasive and unavoidable, it exerts a powerful influence in our lives—exaggerated because hard to recognize. While architecture is probably neither necessary nor sufficient for autonomous living, it is important. When people function autonomously surrounded by architecture that impedes autonomy, they do so in spite of it, overcoming a socio-physical obstacle. When people fail to live autonomously even though their architecture is conducive to it, then there will be countervailing causes. The architecture itself either fosters or discourages the growth and exercise of autonomy.

It might be objected at the outset that I am being cavalier in ignoring the ethical implications of architecture's symbolism. Aside from the immense scope of the topic of architectural symbolism, I put it to one side because our purpose here is to look at more direct influences on autonomy. I wish to deal with the "direct" ethical ramifications of architecture, the way it constrains or enhances our range of autonomous activity, unmediated by its symbolic functioning. To elaborate this view of the direct impact of architecture on our autonomy, I will analyze contemporary American building tendencies and alternatives to them. As with the claims made about the connection between privacy and autonomy, those advanced here have a significant empirical component; therefore, the findings and conclusions of researchers will be cited from time to time.

Architecture influences autonomy in a variety of ways. Most obvious is the way it directly affects our choice and control. More subtle is architecture's influence on our self-concept, scope of social interaction, and degree of individuality. These more subtle influences of architecture impinge on the "substructure" of autonomy: the nature of self and its social relations. What is said in this regard should recall and further our treatment of privacy. Let's begin with what is most evident: that architecture fosters or frustrates autonomy by its immediate effect on our choice and control.

Choice and Control

Architecture exerts a profound influence over our capacities of choice and control by determining two fundamental activities which are also sources of further activity: seeing and moving. Let's start with the way architecture determines what we see. Consider something as easily overlooked as it is obvious—classroom seating design. We are all familiar with the typical arrangement of vertical rows of stationary seats in which all the students face "front," front being where the teacher lectures. Students see the backs of other students and the teacher's front, which means that their options are reduced to one; they can only address and receive response from the teacher. Responses to each other must be bounced off the teacher. She is in charge; the students are virtually powerless.

In decisive contrast is design in which students face one another, such as semi-circular or round-table layouts. Here students can direct comments and questions to each other, or simply look at whomever they please. Because they can choose whom to address or look at, because they have control over the spatial-visual directionality of discussion, they have a subtle form of power. They can function more autonomously than the rows of front-facing students.

Architecture influences autonomy by structuring movement as well as vision. In fact, choice in vision and movement tend to reciprocally determine one another: options in what we see make possible choices in movement, and alternatives in what we can do open up different viewpoints and views. In two apparently minor features of Frank Lloyd Wright's design we see how choice in vision and movement enhances the individual's autonomy. Both involve the way options emerge when space itself is underdetermined.

> In Wright's work, space loses its fixed value and acquires a relative one. [It is] contingent upon the viewer rather than possessing an independent reality of its own. It relates to individuals and their changing position within that space.[1]

One way Wright accomplishes this is by destroying the corners of rooms. Conventional design connects rooms through perpendicularly aligned doors, restricting vision to perpendicular axes. Instead, Wright connects rooms via opened corners, the rooms arranged in diagonal relation to one another. Rather than the predetermined, static visual prospects available in conventional dwellings, Wright's provide more options through more angles of vision. The result is that the individual has more choice in and control over his movement and subsequent experiences. The interplay between choice and movement is even more apparent in a second feature found in many of Wright's designs. The host in the kitchen area (in the Robey house, for example), can, with one step, move from preparing food in screened off privacy to socializing with guests. In this example, freedom of movement translates into visual choice and control. Once again, the spatial design maximizes the individual's autonomy by allowing self-determination rather than determining experience beforehand.

Autonomy is also at stake in the individual's relation to the "outside" built environment, "on the street." In analyzing outdoor plazas, William H. Whyte notes the value of movable chairs in contrast to such fixed seating as benches. The main asset of chairs in public places is movability because movability translates into choice.

> Chairs enlarge choice: to move into the sun, out of it, to make room for groups, move away from them. The possibility of choice is as important as the exercise of it. If you know you can move if you want to, you feel more comfortable staying put.[2]

Whyte goes on to note how people often move a chair just a few inches this way and that, winding up virtually where the chair was to begin with. "The moves are functional, however. They are a declaration of autonomy . . ."[3] As with knowing that we have control over information about ourselves, knowing that we can move the chair we are sitting in strengthens our sense of autonomy by enlarging our sphere of action.

Choice and control over seating doesn't always require the mobility of the artifact itself. We can exercise considerable choice if the built area provides seating (or standing, congregating, moving) options inherently, in its design.

"Choice [in seating] should be built into the basic design. Even though benches and chairs can be added, the best course is to maximize the sittability of inherent features."[4] Thus, Whyte actually counts the number of people sitting around fountains, on ledges, stairs, and walls. No matter how attractive a fountain or plaza, if ready, easy seating isn't available, the area won't be used very frequently. Properly spaced and elevated stairs or ledges, for example, parts of the building or its surroundings that we don't typically think of as "seating," provide people with the sort of built-in option that maximizes choice and thereby makes for lively space.

The use of outdoor areas as habitable space is often overlooked by designers of "institutions." In fact, a hospitably designed outdoors can provide individuals with a valuable choice.

> In residential colleges, tuberculosis sanitoria, Air Force bases, and think-factories, the best places to escape from people are out-of-doors. Landscaping the grounds to provide private places with durable furniture placed in shaded, wooded, hedged areas deserves specific attention.[5]

Sommer's observation also points to the fact, mentioned earlier, that architectural opportunity for autonomy should include privacy options. This is especially important in institutional settings where people usually have less autonomy and privacy than in non-institutional settings.

We can also look at the "big picture:" whole neighborhoods, towns, even cities. Some environs are easy to get around in; in them the individual has a clear sense of where he is because the different spaces hook up with one another in a meaningful pattern. For example, when streets connect in a coherent network, as in central Manhattan's grid or Washington D.C.'s radial design, we are well-oriented in our environment. We know how to get from where we are to where we want to go because we are able to predict what comes in between. Our ability to move easily and efficaciously is directly related to what Kevin Lynch calls "imageability:" the degree to which a city, or sub-unit such as neighborhood or town, enables its inhabitants to visualize its composition.[6] In addition to the coherent street patterns mentioned above, imageability is fostered by such elements as prominent landmarks, thematic districts (such as Manhattan's theatre and diamond districts), and clear borders. The more imageable the environment, the more choice and control the individual has over his movement, the more autonomously he lives.

On the other hand, places that are difficult to picture make inhabitants (and not just visitors) feel confused and tentative. In cities like Jersey City the people are lost among indistinct districts and buildings, ill-defined street patterns, and garbled intersections. Again we see the reciprocal relation between vision and movement. Not only are "unimageable" cities hard to move around in, but obstructions to movement, such as jumbled street design or natural barriers, in turn make imageability difficult.

The same point holds on the micro-level, for smaller units such as buildings. Social psychologist Kiyoshi Izumi finds that architecture can promote feelings of insecurity through visual indeterminacy. He likens the spatial dislocation worry, "Where does the cooridor end? Where does the room end?", to the anxiety experienced when flying in a white-out, "Where does the sky begin and the land start."[7] People experiencing this sort of spatial dislocation will tend to "play it safe," avoiding the anxiety-producing areas, restricting their choices. Their autonomy has been compromised by disorienting interior design.

Researcher Paul Sivadon explains why certain design features make for insecurity by hindering both imageability and vision itself. He notes that the architectures of the French Radio and Television Building creates,

> Strongly insecure space because of the almost total absence of perpendicular axes, helpful in orientation, and the existence of long, circular corridors making any visual survey impossible. You do not know where you are at any moment, or what may happen next.[8]

As these authors indicate, the practical significance of such insecurity is reduction of autonomy. Feelings of insecurity wrought by building design translate into lack of confidence in choice of action, with the result that people actually restrict their movement. What is especially troubling about this is that the cause of their restriction usually goes undetected. Until questioned by a social scientist, most people cannot identify the source of their discomfort or even that they have allowed it to curtail their actions. Since inability to picture movement pattern as well as anticipate experience because of minimized vision goes unnoticed, it is all the more difficult to remedy.

What has been said about imageability needs to be qualified. Although imageability itself enhances autonomy, it may be achieved in such a way as to result in overall loss of autonomy. It can easily be objected that a town or building could be "too" imageable, so "regular" or predictable as to be constricting and actually antagonistic to autonomy. Simplistic imageability could produce what Joan Didion calls, "The architecture of limited possibilities . . . as devoid of privacy or personal eccentricity as the lobby area in the Ramada Inn."[9] Clearly, imageability at the expense of option is not what I am advocating. Fortunately, imageability need not sacrifice variety, interesting detail, individuality of place, even irregularity.

This is because imageability does not mean giving people a pre-packaged picture of their environment; it means building in ways that are *image-able*. The design affords the material from which the individual can fashion her own meaningful picture. Her own purposes, interests, and experiences are integrated with the built particulars. Imageable architecture, therefore, gives the individual the opportunity to exercise her autonomy in creating a subjectively dyed vision of her habitat. An imageable place is open to a variety of interpretations, the way enduring works of art are. This is done, of course, by building options for vision and movement into the details of the area. When choice and control are built into the imageable design, the individual has control over the particular image formed. Just as image-ability of the overall design enhances autonomy, so does choice and control over the image itself.

A good example of imageability-cum-autonomy is Robert Venturi's submission to the Copley Square Competition in Boston, 1966: "An overall, three-dimensional repetitive pattern without a climax."[10] Venturi himself emphasizes the design's contribution to variety of choice in viewpoint, movement, and interpretation. He notes that the main virtue of this apparently boring, repetitive grid, is

> The opportunity for choice and improvisation . . . There are probably more ways to use this square which is 'just a grid' than there are to use those which are interesting, sensitive, and human. And more important, there are more ways to see it.[11]

The lack of central accent, such as a fountain or pond, encourages change in focus so that there are opportunities to see the same thing in different ways. While the grid pattern is conducive to overall imageability, the variety of viewpoint and choice within that pattern ensures that the individual can exercise autonomy in forming his particular image.

The danger of grid design and other symmetrical forms is that even though they provide choice in interpretation and movement, they can frustrate attempts at picturing. So long as the location itself provides means of orientation, as Copley Square's surrounding buildings clearly do, then the Venturi grid can work. But if the context lacks the natural or built forms around which to build our interpretations, then the effect will be disorienting and weaken our autonomy. Underground concourses are often guilty of this. Because they can't draw on surrounding structures or climate, they must completely provide means of pedestrian imaging.

> As environments, subterranean corridors are, for one thing disorienting . . . Part of the trouble is that underground systems are usually laid our symmetrically: North Corridor A is likely to be a mirror image of South Corridor B. Nothing is askew as it is up on the street; there's no landmark on which to get one's bearings, no sun to give a clue to east or west.[12]

Context is crucial. Where it provides for orientation, symmetrical organization *within* it may enhance autonomous activity. But where the repetitive or symmetrical is bereft of such supplementation, it is likely to reduce choice in vision and movement.

Body-Image and Self-Concept

Before leaving the connection between imageability and autonomy, there is one more image to consider—the image we have of our own bodies. Mediating the relationship between architecture and autonomy is the human body. The image we have of our bodies indirectly promotes or erodes our autonomy, and architecture helps shape our body image. Let's turn first, then, to the relationship between body-image and autonomy.

The image we have of our bodies is part of our self-understanding, "The self-image of the body is inseparable from the self-image of the personality."[13] How could it be otherwise when we are in part constituted by our bodies? A strong overall self-concept, therefore, requires a clear image of a capable body. A weak or diminished body-image; however, undermines our overall self-concept. And the weaker our self-concept, the less autonomously do we function. Taken to an extreme, lack of coherent body image is associated with such pathological losses of autonomy as autism.[14] This evidences the importance of body-image to at least a minimally functional self, while also suggesting its role along a continuum of greater range of autonomy.

The significance of body-image to autonomy becomes even more evident in light of the role our bodies play in our "public" self-concept. Our bodies are the public presentations of our selves. It is through and by means of our bodies that we experience the public world and that world experiences us. A strong sense of body is needed to imaginatively project ourselves acting in the public arena. Along with control over our bodies, "developing accurate body images . . . are indispensable for the building of the self-image that will permit the individual to see himself in relation to the world outside."[15] A robust body-image, therefore, is an essential ingredient in our concept of self as public actor. And seeing ourselves as public actors is crucial to acting autonomously since the quality of self-concept helps determine the scope and nature of action.

Architecture relates to us immediately as embodied beings—another sense in which it is public. When we move through and around buildings, we are not only experiencing the architecture by means of our bodies, but are experiencing our bodies by means of the architecture. Scurrying down a narrow, steeply pitched corridor, for example, is somatically rather different from the experience of ascending a gradual spiral, such as found in the Guggenheim Museum. The way our built environment invites or rebuffs our bodies fashions the way we feel and picture ourselves in the public world: as energetic and effective, or dulled and powerless.

Environmental design can enhance our body-image. By welcoming motor exploration and rewarding perception it "draws our bodies out," and keeps us "in touch." Consider J. B. Jackson's description of the "marvelous sequence" of experiences afforded by New York City's Grand Central Terminal:

> Emerging in a dense, slow-moving crowd from the dark, cool, low-ceilinged platform, he suddenly enters the immense concourse with its variety of heights and levels, and the smooth texture of its floors and walls. Almost every sense is stimulated and flattered; even posture and gait are momentarily improved.[16]

But the Grand Central Terminal seems the exception in contemporary American architecture. Too much of our built environment offends the senses and discourages movement.

When architecture is repeatedly indifferent or hostile to our bodies, we experience our bodies as cumbersome, awkward, or simply as the source of discomfort. This is disembodying design in the sense that it makes us want to disown our bodies; they are not to be enjoyed or trusted. Consider the increasing number of huge, box-like, glass buildings. Their lack of functional, visual, and motor orientation produces a sense of impenetrability. We immediately feel somehow at a "disadvantage" upon approaching these buildings; dwarfed and disoriented, we are often at a loss for action. When the built environment conspires to convey a negative, meager body-image; therefore, it is difficult to conceive of ourselves as autonomous, capable of purposeful action in the world outside. By attacking our body-image, numbing places like State Street in Chicago undermine our autonomy. "Affronted by the noise and the crowds; a monotonous dead-level surface is underfoot, and a monotonous geometric perspective stretches in either direction; monotonous facades line on either side."[17]

Because our self-concept is conditioned by the experience we have of our own bodies, it shrinks to fit its felt bodily proportions, as, "the mental functions correspond to the image the organism has of its relation to the world . . ."[18] Disorienting, disembodying architecture attacks our body-image which in turn detracts from an autonomous self-concept in general. Because our bodies are the public presentations of our selves, diminution in the sense we have of ourselves as public performers is a natural consequence of disembodying architecture.

Social Interaction and Autonomy

Social interaction contributes to autonomy in at least two ways: as an option for the exercise of autonomy; and as a necessary or enabling condition of its exercise. The first adds a significant, if not essential, domain for autonomous choice. The latter is more like education or transportation; it makes possible autonomous functioning that would not otherwise exist.

That social interaction is one of the choices available to autonomous people seems obvious enough. Just as we can choose to work or relax, read or listen to music, so can we choose to be with others. But as an option, its importance to autonomy cuts deeper. Without the opportunity to be with others, autonomy is empty. Autonomy derives its meaning from a social context in that we exercise autonomy in relation to others, as social beings. It seems ironic or jejune to describe someone alone on a desert island as autonomous. The converse seems equally dismal. Social interaction without control over when and with whom one is to interact is oppressive—as in such total institutions as prisons, hospitals, and the military. We lack autonomy, then, when either forced to intereact or denied it as an option. Social interaction and autonomy complement one another: each without the other is sorely deficient.

A. *Social Interaction, An Option for Autonomy*

The emphasis on movement at the expense of pause and congregation, most obvious in accommodations to the automobile, bespeaks a growing tendency to create "dead" public spaces,[19] spaces that cut us off from one another. This is especially insidious because these kinds of public spaces often appear to provide social amenities—as with certain playgrounds, streets, and shopping centers. Seeing people "in" or "using" these areas, we are too apt to conclude that they are satisfactory. But, typically, their design either keeps people apart or hurries them on their way. Because pedestrians are treated as people going to or from a car, we miss or ignore opportunities to design spaces that promote social gathering and interaction.

The Brunswick Centre in the Bloomsbury section of London provides Richard Sennett with a telling example. Its central concourse is an area to pass through rather than use. The few shops and vast areas of empty space do not create a sense of expansiveness (the way New York's Grand Central Terminal does), but instead produce a sense of being lost and isolated. "To sit on one of the few concrete benches in the concourse for any length of time is to become profoundly uncomfortable, as though one were on exhibit in a vast empty hall."[20] The real purpose of this "Centre" is to provide a pass-through area from car or bus to office. The architecture produces social isolation without physical separation because, "the public space has become a derivative of movement."[21]

This example parallels the more ubiquitous one of city sidewalk width. After noting how important wide sidewalks are for social interaction and especially children's play, Jane Jacobs observes how, "sidewalk width is invariably sacrificed for vehicular width, partly because city sidewalks are conventionally considered to be purely *space for pedestrian travel and access to buildings*,"[22] rather than *places* in their own right. When sidewalks are trimmed down to make wider streets for automobile traffic, we lose crucial areas of congregation, play, discussion, and interest. Public places of pause and gathering are, perhaps unwittingly, sacrificed to economy of movement.

Architecture can isolate socially, however, without separating us physically. This is evidenced in the structuring of vision in some contemporary office design. Many large offices such as those found in insurance companies or corporate headquarters are designed as huge open spaces with no walls or partitions. Sometimes a set of private offices for administrators rings the perimeter of this vast expanse. The effects include social isolation and silence: "When everyone has each other under surveillance, sociability decreases, silence being the only form of protection."[23] Loss of visual privacy, achieved through multiple reciprocal viewing, yields circumspection and withdrawal. Some office planners claim that this open space plan increases worker efficiency because people are less likely to gossip or "goof off" when exposed to one another—and their superiors.

Other business people, however, take the opposite view and think that socializing increases productivity. *Business Week* (October 4, 1982) reports that Michael A. Brunner, a vice-president at the Eastern Regional Headquarters of A.T.&T., claims that " 'the building enhances the productivity of our total team.' The interior courts and vaulted atrium of the project . . . foster contact among workers,' Brunner says. " 'People see more of each other. I can't prove it, but I know it improves our effectiveness.' " The interior courts invite social intimacy by enclosing the visual space; at the same time, the airy, light prospect afforded by the vaulted atrium gives a sense of freedom. Together they foster social interaction, an interaction that at least some administrators find productive.

When we design space which invites social interaction we facilitate the collective, social exercise of autonomy. The medieval courtyard and some contemporary condominium designs illustrate how buildings can be organized to create "living" public space. The medieval courtyard, for example, brought together entertainment, street trades, cafes, and shops. It thereby provided a focus for public social life, inviting assembly and transaction. In the rebuilding of London, which took place in the late seventeenth century, city squares were designed expressly to repel such congregation, to keep the lower classes from the shared thought and action which can result in the collective exercise of autonomy. (The degree to which politics is embedded in architecture was not lost on *these* urban planners.)

Most obvious in much contemporary condominium planning, especially in the South, are the large central meeting houses or poolside areas. But more crucial and less conspicuous is the court-like design of the dwelling space: a central area about which attached or semi-attached homes are arrayed. Entrances to the homes face this courtyard so that the many daily comings and goings tend to be shared with neighbors. These casual, everyday occasions to see, be seen, and get to know one another foster a sense of communal life and common control over a commonly enjoyed environment. The inward-facing design helps make the condominium dwellers into a distinctive community, even though they themselves may be the last to recognize how this is coming about.

But neither the medieval nor the condominium courtyard typifies the design of most "living" space in America today. Instead, people tend to live anonymously in large apartment buildings or insular private homes. Most apartment housing defeats social interaction in two ways: within, linear corridor design is not conducive to routine socializing; without, the relationship among the separately conceived buildings tends to create an unplanned residue of space, not surprisingly — "dead" public space. William L. Yancey argues that the lack of "semi-public space" in the (now defunct) Pruitt-Igoe Housing Project (St. Louis, Missouri) atomized its occupants, preventing the formation of community. What architects and urban planners have often injudiciously considered "wasted space" (space within or between buildings that is outside individual dwelling units), in fact provides a locus for shared activity. The semi-public stairwells and corridors of Pruitt-Igoe were not adequate to facilitate informal social networks. On the contrary,

> The design of stairwells [in Pruitt-Igoe] is such that they represent almost completely uncontrollable space. They are public in the sense that anyone can enter them without being challenged, yet they are private in that no one is likely to be held accountable for his behavior in the stairwell."[24]

So, what semi-public spaces *were* created in the building of Pruitt-Igoe, were merely unplanned leftovers which fostered delinquent rather than communal behavior. Rather than romantically lament the passing of the slums which gave way to projects like Pruitt-Igoe, Yancey observes that in "traditional" lower-class neighborhoods:

> Alleys, streets, and backyards provide the ecological basis around which informal networks of friends and relations may develop. Without such semi-public space and facilities, the development of such networks is retarded.[25]

Neglect, vandalism, debris, and violence are traceable to this lack of community. And while the failure to provide semi-public places of social interaction is not alone responsible, it contributes mightily.

Robert Sommer calls attention to a similar problem writ small, in high school design.

> High schools provide few places for students to linger, so they congregate in the corridors, outside the locker rooms, or in the stairwells seeking refuge from crowd pressure and impersonal, authority.[26]

The moral of this story is that people need options for social interaction, sometimes in private settings. When they are not architecturally provided for, then they will "improvise" as best they can.

On the other hand, the increased *privacy* of the private house is epitomized by the disappearance of that once traditional home-extension, the front porch. This is unfortunate because the screened-in porch carries unnoticed social significance. It dissolves the wall between private place and public space, inviting the communal life which is built on easy, spontaneous social interacton. The semi-public nature of the porch affords our autonomy great latitude in determining levels of intimacy: from a greeting of recognition to a brief chat or more extended, indoor discussion. But with air-conditioning and the back yard barbecue orientation, we lose this casual sharing of space and with it cultivation of that unit of communal autonomy, the neighborhood.

B. Social Interaction as Facilitating Autonomy

Let us now take up the way in which social interaction actually facilitates or provides a necessary condition for the exercise of our autonomy. Social interaction makes both personal (non-social) as well as shared (communal) choices available that would otherwise be closed off. Connection with other people can both increase our range of choice and provide us with the means of exerting control over the larger, public circumstances of life. In discussing sidewalk contact, Jane Jacobs points out that the most important factor determining city vitality is casual, everyday, public interaction. In the course of their daily comings and goings, people stop and exchange ideas with the result that their arises, "a feeling for the public identity of people, a web of public respect and trust, and a resource in time of personal or neighborhood need."[27]

When public interaction and the concomitant sense of community exists, we gain in autonomy at the very least because the streets are safer. We are free to move about as we wish. When interaction and sense of neighborhood are lacking, the street dangers curtail our freedom. Jacobs illustrates this by contrasting two sides of the same street in New York's East Harlem.

On the project side of the street across the way, the children, who had a fire hydrant open beside their play area, were behaving destructively, drenching the open windows of houses with water, squirting it on adults . . . Nobody dared to stop them. These were anonymous children . . . What if you scolded or stopped them? Who would back you up? Impersonal city streets make anonymous people; it is a matter of what kinds of tangible enterprises sidewalks have, and therefore of how people use sidewalks in practical everyday life.[28]

Public social interactions and the relations they spawn also enhance the scope of our autonomy in more personal ways, for instance, by providing such informal services as parcel drops, newspaper saving, and key leaving.

When a friend wants to use our place while we are away for a weekend, he can pick up the key at the delicatessen across the street. Joe Comacchia, who keeps the delicatessen, usually has a dozen or so keys at a time for handing out like this.[29]

Jacobs goes on to remark that these sorts of services cannot be formalized lest the recipient's privacy be transgressed. Such transgression, of course, would diminish autonomy. These informal services and the social relations on which they are based arise because of public street life. And such life grows out of the arrangements of physical space and social place. Ideally, as Jacobs demonstrates over and over, there is diversity: diversity of people, of schedules, of use, of structure. When residences, stores, office buildings, parks, and schools mix, street life bustles. The publicly formed relationships which enlarge our autonomy are built on something as simple yet precarious as the mixed use which brings together delicatessen and apartment building.

However, when streets are designed homogeneously, for example, with nothing but residences, "people must enlarge their private lives if they are to have anything approaching equivalent contact with neighbors."[30] But this increased social interaction requires loss of privacy, as private relationships expand beyond desirability. Autonomy in one direction is then gained at its cost in another. This illustrates how the public and private are not in "opposition" to one another, but are reciprocally related. On Jacobs' interpretation, stronger public life makes for more, not less, privacy.

The following example reveals how architecture can obstruct the shared, communal exercise of autonomy by determining social interaction. The obstructions to social give and take occur in the effects on movement and vision. Several years ago, our philosophy department moved from a building with a central large office, from which individual offices radiated, to one in which offices are aligned along three "blind" corridors joined at right angles to one another. We became physically isolated from one another as this corridor arrangement inhibits informal fraternizing. In moving from a "hub and spokes" arrangement to a frame pattern, we lost a natural locus of congregation, and with it ease in the sharing of ideas, questioning, and criticizing that such casual gathering entails. This is the very kind of interaction, however, which increases the autonomy of each by promoting collective thought and decision-making on a daily, unplanned basis. Free access to others in the group translates into greater group and individual control over departmental matters.

The philosophy department lost what Humphry Osmond calls "sociopetality": "That quality [of built design] which encourages, fosters, and even enforces the development of stable interpersonal relationships."[31] It was replaced by a "centrifugal" design, one which tends to prevent the formation of relationships. It is not surprising that Osmond cites the circular medical wards at the Liverpool Royal Infirmary in England as sociopetal, in contrast to the linear corridor design of most hospitals, prisons, and old age homes. The Philosophy Department, in effect, traded the sociopetality of the hub and spokes arrangement, for the corridor-frame design typical of most large care facilities.

One serious consequence of this for autonomy is that the chairman now tends to poll individuals separately instead of the department members informally discussing policy together. This means that only the chairman has access to all opinions, and then, taken only separately. It also means that the habits of shared self-reflection and deliberation, constitutive of collective autonomy, are not furthered on an everyday basis by the lay-out of the offices. Social interaction proceeds, of course, but *in spite of* rather than *because* of the architecture. A radical *communal* alteration in the functioning of the Philosophy Department is thus wrought by a fundamental change in architectural design—resulting in a greater formality in regularly scheduled meetings, and a disturbing proliferation of memo-sending.

Individuality and Place

So far we have seen how architecture affects autonomy by determining choice and control and our range of social interaction. In addition, it affects autonomy by encouraging or blunting the development of our individuality: the degree to which our identities are distinctive. Throughout this book, the self has been examined, primarily in terms of the abilities and capacities that constitute autonomy or directly contribute to it. Thus, we discussed reasoning ability, self-control, and self-knowledge. Here I'd like to broaden the purview just a bit and discuss more general abilities and capacities—those which define us as individuals. This will have an indirect bearing on our autonomy. The more of a distinctive self we are, the more there is a defined "subject" of autonomy, hence, the more depth and solidity to the autonomy enjoyed. Personal identity is the center from which autonomous thought and action spring. Among the capacities and abilities which define us as individuals are our senses and imagination, what we might call our "appreciative" faculties.

Through the exercise and development of these faculties we are shaped as this or that particular person. The more we are informed by our senses, the more we are animated by our imagination, the more of a self there is to be autonomous. Of course, acute perception and lively imagination also contribute to autonomy more directly by disclosing possibilities of thought, choice, and action. As pointed out in Chapter 1, habits of perception and imagination are embedded in our reasoning and choosing. What I shall argue in this section is that architecture enriches or impoverishes our individuality by its effect on our appreciative faculties, in particular by creating or failing to create "place." The individuality of place helps individualize *us* as people (much as we develop by interacting with people with strong personalities). Through the development of our appreciative faculties, the identity of place enlarges our personal identities, whereas "placeless" design diminishes us by blunting these faculties.

I am using "place" as an honorific or achievement term. Many areas or spaces fail to be places in the sense here intended. Place is akin to John Dewey's sense of "an" (aesthetic) experience: *that* particular meal, outing, ballgame. A distinctive event which stands out in our memory. A place is a portion of our surroundings that has a personality, an identity of its own. It invites us and provides opportunity for autonomous living. We relate to places in ways that create meaning, whereas placeless space is unresponsive to our inhabiting endeavors.

Rober Sommer sees our need to make spaces our "own" by exercising control over them as basic to our human nature:

> There is a lesson to be learned when executives put calendars and charts on the backs of glass doors, college students choose old barracks over modern dormitories . . . People like spaces they can call their own and make over; they reject an alien environment that is built according to detailed square footage allocations for a standard model of impersonal humanity in the most durable and antiseptic condition.[32]

Sommer goes on to suggest that uniformity and drabness in design will eventually reduce our capacity to respond to the environment. Of course, different structures provide different *kinds* of places. We don't expect the same experience or scope for our autonomy in a concert hall as we do in our house. But some concert halls manage to be places and other don't, and we don't feel at home in all houses.

We grow by appropriating the particularity of place sensuously and imaginatively. It challenges us to discriminate among details, ferreting out what is important and harbors ramifications. Place sensitizes us to nuance and change. At the same time we are called upon to unify the diverse elements, to see how they hang together in ways that we are not accustomed to. The identity of a place derives in part from its relation to its context. We are thereby induced by place to trace connections with different facets of the surrounding environment.

Place develops our appreciative faculties by encouraging us to envisage possibilities of design, vision, and movement. We not only want to explore and "use" the space of place, but we want to try it out in our imaginations. The personality of place requires that we adjust to it in interesting, innovative ways. When we confront the distinctive personality of a true place, therefore, we are not permitted simply to recognize forms and classify images in a passive, reactive way. We cannot pass over detail and form once we have ascertained their functional role. But this is what placeless architecture does; it does not challenge or enliven our appreciative faculties. It dulls them and fosters automatic, inattentive reactions. By diminishing our powers of perception and imagination, placeless design diminishes our very selves. Shrinking personal identity in turn reduces the "base" from which autonomous thought and action proceed.

Placelessness is due to a variety of features of built space. Architecture that is standardized in its design creates homogeneous space, space without individuality. In order for built space to have an identity it must have individuating characteristics, features that define it as this particular place. For this we need architectural individuality. In addition, place requires that the architecture be situated and so situate us in a particular context. But placeless design fails to connect with context. Context is comprised of several dimensions; spatial, temporal, and socio-cultural. Space is both natural and built. As noted above, our experience of nature is largely determined by the way our spaces are built. Context also includes time, our sense of the time of day and year, as well as of time passing. Lastly, place provides a socio-cultural pattern of activity and interest. For context is not simply a physical thing, it includes social action, human interests, and meaning.

To make my case, I will look at a few types of buildings which seem typical of the growing trend toward placeless architecture in America. I will conclude with an extended examination of shopping malls. Malls seem to be paradigmatic, despite their relatively recent appearance on the scene. They are the culmination of nowhere design because so comprehensive in their effect. What I am offering, then, is a brief critique of a tendency in contemporary architecture. The critique is both aesthetic and ethical, since concerned with the impact of built design on our individuality and autonomy.

A. Architectural Individuality

America is blanketed by standardized architecture, architecture that lacks individuality of design. As a result we are spending more of our time in homogeneous space. It doesn't matter where we are, we will see big, box-like office buildings whose facades are blank walls or equally impenetrable mirrors. Regardless of the virtues of such construction, the debilitating thing about these buildings is their sameness from region to region, town to town. They tend not to have faces—entryways that are human in scale and invite us in. They tend to have large, disorienting lobbies. The same bland textures and colors, lighting and rectilinear geometry, make them virtually identical.

The same is true of motels and restaurants. The blessing of the franchise is its guarantee of sameness regardless of region. Several years ago Holiday Inn came up with the slogan—"No Surprises!" They turned an apparent liability, monotonous sameness of design, into a virtue. One Holiday Inn is just like the next, and we love this. Why? It must be because we are insecure in our travelling. The spirit of adventure and exploration has left us and we flee the unknown. We flee to the safety of the familiar. But in such flight we lose a condition of individual growth, the challenge to our senses and imagination that deepens their reach. These are the faculties of appreciation, called forth when we find ourselves interacting with individualized design and individuated space.

It isn't just that Holiday Inns are all over and all look and feel the same. It's also that there are virtually no architectural differences among the different franchises. Holdiay Inn, Best Western, Ramada Inn, what's the difference? With our eyes closed we can tell where the front desk, restaurant, swimming pool, and gameroom will be. There are no surprises. Yet surprise keeps us on our toes, on the lookout for the implicit meaning, alert to possibility. No surprises may be something of a gain, but the loss is profound for all its unobtrusiveness.[33]

We can clarify the trend toward placeless design by contrasting current building tendencies with what they are replacing. Let's begin with the change in the design of movie theatres. Compare the old-fashioned movie theatre with contemporary multiplex structures. The free-standing movie house, whether in major city or small town, is distinctive among its neighboring buildings. It is big. It has a big lobby, provides a big air space above our heads, and shows its images on a big screen. The movie house shines in the night, sparkling with strings of light proclaiming the theatre's name, embellishing the marquee, and announcing the current fare. It promises the magic of a night out. Even before the film begins, its ornate, rococo architecture and star-studded, heavenly balcony usher us into another world. The theatre stands alone, marked off as a special place which offers larger than life people and drama. We can identify with it because it has an identity of its own.

The multiplex movie building can't really be called a "theatre." It's just another business, with no special decor or architectural character. The design of its exterior does little to reveal the cinematic purpose of the building. Often embedded in a series of similar structures, the multiplex cinema looks like a small office building. We're not in a separate bulding, marking off a separate space. The screen and the viewing room itself are usually cut down, mini-sized.

The movie rooms are packaged two, four, six, even twelve to a slab. The result is that the symbolic, celebratory nature of the theatre is destroyed. Movies are reduced to commodities, as movie-going becomes another purchase rather than a festive occasion with its own rituals and contours. Of course, the packaging of movies as video-cassettes domesticates film viewing still further, but that's yet another story.

B. Spatial Context: Architectural and Natural

In addition to individuating architecture, place requires connection with context. Spatial environment is the most obvious dimension of context when discussing architecture, so let's begin with it. Standardized architecture is to be expected where there is no architectural context to play off of or where context is decidedly ignored. Without the moorings provided by architectural context, the design of buildings tends to be dictated by common, levelling considerations; and this results in a common, homogeneous package. We can see this in the supplanting of the neighborhood ballpark. Stadiums and whole sport complexes are being built in empty suburban spaces which afford access to expressways and plenty of parking. Their design tends to be symmetrical, with even, clean lines. The addition of elaborate scoreboards or visual attractions, such as the waterfalls in Kansas City's Truman Complex, are thought to contribute some character. But these decorations can't overcome the barrenness of the setting or the standard form of the building. Little local texture is generated because the structure itself really isn't located in a particular built context. Consequently its form doesn't bespeak a traditional locale.

In contrast, neighborhood or "urban" ballparks are usually bursting with architectural individuality because they are informed by their physical surroundings. They had their contours "determined by their insertion in the existing urban grid, so each park was the outcome of a dialogue between the spatial requirements of the field and the spatial limitations imposed by the site."[34] Each park had to adapt to the idiosyncrasies of its place in the larger scheme of city life. This resulted in asymmetrical layouts, replete with design features as distinctive as a person's signature. Fenway Park, for instance, has a huge left field wall with a screen attached "to prevent home runs from beaning pedestrians and breaking windows across the street."[35]

The architectural style of these ballparks was typically dictated by the surrounding city structures. Thus, Ebbets field in Brooklyn was marked by its brick Renaissance facade with Corinthian capitals and arched windows. And, "Comiskey Park in Chicago . . . adopted a virile warehouse vocabulary appropriate to the city, and enlivened it with geometric decoration reminiscent of Frank Lloyd Wright's Prairie Style."[36] No such context of architectural pressure or presence informs the building of contemporary, exurban stadia. Answering only to the demands of efficiency, cleanliness, and mass accessibility, they turn out to look and feel very much the same.

The domed stadium carries this contextlessness one step further. True, the domed stadium provides protection and a guaranteed outing. But the dome cuts us off from the natural and built environment whose distinctive features situate us in a particular time and place. What I am calling the neighborhood ballpark affords a distinctive perspective on the outside world of buildings and hills, rivers and roads, sky and stars. We know we are somewhere. As Neilson nicely points out, what we see in the neighborhood may be replete with the cultural identity of the particular place. "From Sportman's Park in St. Louis, fans could see Romanesque brick spires of churches that revealed the city's large central-European population."[37]

No one can deny the pleasure and convenience of watching a sporting event free of wind or rain, heat and humidity. But the domed arena is antiseptic and the baseball or football game becomes denatured. The game space feels shrunken because it is closed off above, and the artificial turf looks like a big billiards table. The odors of people and nature mingling are gone. The steady purr of air-conditioning replaces outdoor noises, and the sound of bat meeting ball, for instance, is muted. In the case of football, the enclosure removes nature as a major means of testing and differentiating teams. Over the years, certain teams have been characteristically tough amidst the adversity of the elements. The Green Bay Packers and Chicago Bears are especially intimidating in snow and bitter wind. As more teams take their act indoors, we will lose at least this ingredient in their distinctive personalities.

Finally, the domed stadium exacerbates the tendency of sports to lose their seasonal identities. Free of climatic constraints, baseball can be played deep into autumn and football in summer or spring. Thus, sports lose their seasonal niches, and with that their own time in the annual cycle. When any sport can be played anytime, we are in danger of forgetting their distinctive personalities and the way their differences harmonize in the yearly round of play. As the sports we watch become uprooted in time, so do we. As we shall see, temporal dislocation also contributes to placelessness.

C. Total Isolation—The Mall

The enclosed shopping mall carries the idea of the domed stadium one step further. Not just a sporting event, but a world of commodities, displays, and people is vouched safe for us. Malls are convenient, all the shops together, so close and easy to get at. Of course getting to the mall requires a car. But the mall itself turns it back on the car and road, shutting out their noise, dirt, and danger. It thereby provides the boon of a purely pedestrian domain, especially attractive as a setting in which the young and old can exercise and otherwise enjoy "protected" space. The very insulation of the mall, however, also isolates it. This isolation results in isolating us, the mall-goers, from the various contexts which yield a sense of place. We shall see how the mall lacks the architectural individuality and spatial context just noted in contemporary movie theatres and ballparks. In addition, the typical mall fails to situate us socially and temporally.

1. SPACE AND SOCIO-CULTURAL CONTEXT

The mall is placeless because it is nowhere; it is nowhere because it could be anywhere. Usually, the mall is created *ex nihilo*: out of nothing—uninhabited, empty space. It is plopped down anywhere, any field, any desert plot, any vacant lot (provided studies show consumers can get there and will go). But because nowhere and because totally insulated, the mall is not part of a spatial context. As a result, its environment is disconnected from surrounding space, both natural and man-made. An enclosed self-sufficient world, the mall seals us mall-goers off from the rest of the world. When we are no longer of this land, this town, this region, we lose a terrain in which individuality can take root. Integration with spatial context provides a strong source of place, and with this particularizing of space a focus for our individuating powers.

Urban malls and other enclosed "megastructures" have the advantage of an architectural context with which to interact. Most, however, ignore their surroundings. Detroit's Renaissance Center and Atlanta's Omni International wall out the street with an impenetrable concrete or brick facade. This doesn't have to be. The I.D.S. Center in Minneapolis is a large, enclosed space that works because, "psychologically as well as visually, the Center has an excellent relationship with the street and surroundings. They are eminently visible, and this helps make pedestrian flow easy."[38] Visual and motor access to its surroundings, situates the I.D.S. building in a particular place, providing specific orientation for its clients. But this building is by far the exception, bucking the trend toward placelessness.

Mall life has no local texture or meaning; it has no location. This dislocates us mall-goers in very subtle ways, ways of which we are probably unaware. There is no sense of history, of religion, of anything other than shopping in the mall. While it's a blessing to be safe from weather, it's also a curse in that climate gives us a sense of being somewhere in particular. Whether a drizzly Seattle fall or a biting Chicago winter, climate locates us in both season and region.

Moreover, architectural adaptations to climate and topography heighten our sense of being in *this* place, with its details, rather than somewhere else. Airy balconies are suited to New Orleans' sultry climate, but wrong for

Minneapolis. The stucco homes that hug the ground in southern Florida are out of place in New England. But the structure of malls rarely reflects locale, with the result that most malls look and feel alike.

One thing we easily overlook is that built and natural contexts are not merely physical. They also locate and structure our interests, purposes, and activities. Cut off from the rest of our spatial environment, the typical mall severs our connection with the larger community. The mall exists in a vacuum, without a socio-cultural context. Not really a mini-community, the mall is more a commodities coalition. It is disconnected from the other (non-shopping) activities of our lives, activities that go on in offices, schools, parks, libraries, and residences. As a result, what goes on in the mall is not integrated with the rest of our environment or life.

Life in the mall helps define us merely in terms of commodities and consumer interests, suppressing the other values and interests which individualize us. This is a force for personal fragmentation. It is reasonable to think that the more our diverse desires, habits, and values are integrated, the more we are individualized as *this* particular person (this was seen to be a dimension of autonomy itself in Chapter 1). Insofar as mall life works against such integration by separating various activities and interests from shopping, it weakens our individuality.

2. ARCHITECTURAL INDIVIDUALITY

Mall architecture and the space it creates tend to be similar no matter where we are. As remarked in discussing stadium design, buildings tend toward standardized forms when not responsive to their spatial context. (Idiosyncratic form, the other extreme, is much rarer, for a variety of reasons.) The architecture of malls is usually not adapted to the built or natural surroundings because it doesn't have to be. A mall in Houston could just as easily be in Atlanta or Seattle.

Malls are usually laid out in a basic pattern. Two crossing axes are "anchored" at their ends by large department stores such as Sears or Macy's. Conduits of movement are also standardized. The walkways and paths tend to be arranged around some central core. The stores form a perimeter and we are encouraged to walk around this core (empty space, fountain, stairways, escalators). What is also the same from mall to mall is the way this layout keeps us moving. Rarely is the core itself a place to congregate the way plaza, courtyard or park are. The benches don't face one another, but are lined up so that when we sit we see store windows rather than each other (which makes good merchandising sense). Where an occasional bench or space does permit pause and interaction, we must fight the curent of incessant movement.

Mall space is homogeneous, moreover, because the stores are interchangeable. Not only do we find the same stores or their clones from one mall to the next, but the store functions are remarkably similar. The samenesss in their functions is revealed by what is missing. No grocery stores or tailor shops or shoe repairs. No flavor of local ownership, but the blandness of franchise—managers rather than owners. But even this is not what is most importantly the same from mall to mall.

What's most palpably the same is the mall ambience and space: the "easy-listening" music, the potted trees, the regularity of space and spacing. The mall is characterized by even storefronts, small facades, and close groupings of stores.[39] An architect of malls, Cesar Peli, recognizes that there are no *interstices*, no spaces separating stores; the nooks and crannies, alleys and alcoves, that a downtown provides. This is a great loss, for these little nodules of apparent emptiness are also distinctive places of personal identification and social gathering.

In the mall, we are immersed in the milky lighting and muffled sound, as an overall hum permeates because the sounds of walking and talking are kept in to reverberate, mingle, and become indistinct. The aesthetic of mall space seduces us into easy-going strolling from store to store. The effortless, hushed rhythm of gliding and shopping, shopping and gliding, tranquilizes us. We are entranced by the susurrus of movement. All this remains the same even if store names change. Going into a new mall, we don't even have to pay attention to names. The familiar rhythms of traffic patterns, merchandising, and transaction draw us in and out like a hot breath.

3. TIME

Contributing to the placelessness of malls is their timeless quality. Not only does the mall lack a history of its own, but we have no sense of time inside the mall. In the mall, we are deprived of the natural temporal cues which real places provide.[40] We don't feel the air warming up or cooling down. Neither do we feel or hear prevailing winds start to blow or change direction. A real place imprints its own features on how we read nature: the lengthening of shadows cast by particular buildings, the way a river or lake changes hue in the course of the day. But in the mall, we glide along in artificial light or natural light that's so refracted and reflected as to be of no help at all as far as time goes. Our senses are deprived of the natural events which evoke an awareness of particular times as well as of temporality in general.

In downtown life, we also have a pastiche of human activity by which to gauge the passing of time. We tell time by sensing traffic patterns and the time it takes to go from one place to another. In larger cities, in fact, when someone asks how far away a place is, we usually answer in terms of time, not distance.[41] Time is indicated by the daily rhythm of school letting out, lunch break, rush hour. Our own activities and the time it takes to engage in them give our days a pace by which we temporally orient ourselves.

But in the mall time stands still, no distinctive events punctuate and delineate a discernible tempo. We float for hours without seeing a clock. Our own exertions, tasks, or errands, are hardly enough to yield a sense of time. The most difficult thing we do is try on clothing. We drift along, moving easily, mesmerized by the merchandise, soothed by the sound of reverberating voices and Muzak. To live timelessly is to lose an essential dimension of human existence. To sense time passing is to feel *our* time elapsing, to be in touch with the temporality of human life. Our identity is bound up with this temporal self-consciousness. To lose touch with this is to be hollowed out.

4. DOWNTOWN

To underscore what this all means, let's contrast the mall more fully with a downtown area in city or town, the very thing malls compete with and often replace. In a real downtown there are distinctive landmarks. We are oriented by and to parks, plazas, statues, locally owned trade shops, offices, maybe adjoining schools or libraries, and residences. There is variety in ground cover: cement, blacktop, brick, cobblestone, gravel, grass. And the architecture is diverse. Different periods and styles are represented because they were not built all at once, the way a mall is. Diverse architectural materials complement this heterogeneity in style and function. The buldings are of different heights, textures, shapes, and sizes. Even the streets may be laid out irregularly, with their little quirks and cul-de-sacs. Thus we move between different kinds of space. Broad promenades give way to winding alleys; skyscrapers alternate with small shops and parks; and pedestrian sanctuaries open onto traffic.

The aesthetic richness of this sort of environment stimulates our senses and calls upon our imagination. By eliciting a range of responses, environmental variety enlivens our appreciative powers, thereby developing our individuality. The complexity of downtown life also makes demands on our powers of integration and adaptation. We must integrate the wealth of detail and variation upon pain of being overwhelmed. And we must adapt our perception and behavior to often abrupt or disturbing changes in the surroundings: a traffic accident; a group of running children; a sudden cloudburst. This adaptation and integration deepens and defines us.

On the other hand, the mall is desensitizing. It blunts our faculties of appreciation by providing a surrounding which discourages discriminating perception. The blandness of the mall's sensory diet weakens our sensitivity to individuality when we do encounter it. Because the senses feed the imagination, moreover, desensitized people tend to suffer an impoverishment of imagination.[42]

A downtown has an identity. Consequently we can identify with it and this thereby helps define and enrich our own identities. A genuine downtown provides pockets of meanings, meanings we help bestow by virtue of our interaction with the places and with each other in the places it provides. This corner, that restaurant, this drugstore. Places to meet and be together. They become meaningful over time, as we walk home from school or work and stop in for a pop or beer. Gradually, over time, in the midst of a spectrum of activities (including shopping), spaces become places. We share our histories with them; we grow up together. And just as some of us move away and others come, so too in a real downtown, buildings, and stores change function, get torn down, get put up. But not all at once, and not in a homogeneous, prefabricated way. It is just because of such co-temporaneous construction that even when old, malls don't really have histories.

What I have offered is a generalization. Some malls do build-in aspects of a local identity, just as some contemporary hotels, theatres, and stadia have real personalities of their own. But this kind of architecture requires imagination and effort, for it swims against the tide—the tendency of built public space to placelessness. Because insulated and isolated, it is natural for malls especially to be nowhere in particular. This, I suggest, threatens to erode our identities, as we become no one in particular.

As I have tried to show, the creation of place is but one way in which architecture can contribute to autonomy. Providing for choice and control, robust body-images, and opportunities for social interaction also enhance our autonomy. When architecture fails to do this it is especially threatening because it is especially difficult to notice. Architecture in general, whether good or bad, is like the air we breathe or the language we speak; so pervasive as to be unremarkable. But when it obstructs autonomy, architecture is also self-concealing and self-perpetuating. This is because autonomy is the very thing needed to diagnose the problem and improve our built environment. By impeding the exercise and development of autonomy, much contemporary architecture keeps us from the thought, imagination, and action needed to remedy the conditions which thwart autonomy.

Conclusion

The treatment of the topics in this book has been governed by an "educational" perspective. The discussion of each issue is to some extent concerned with the education of the capacities which make for autonomous living. This is brought out most explicitly in the last chapter by addressing the edifying nature of edifices. But different kinds of edification are also found in the family, in the varieties of respectful treatment, and the granting of privacy. Each in its own way builds up the independence of thought and action, the habits of reflection and choice, which make us autonomous. Conversely, this book has also been about miseducation—the relationships and practices which constrict or deaden our capacities for self-governance. Fostering dependence (whether our own or another's), lying, as well as deprivation of privacy and physical "place," conspire to limit our powers for autonomous living. They either deprive us of the necessary educational medium or actually miseducate and mislead our habits of thinking and acting.

Autonomous living is good. It is good for other valuable experiences and relationships, and it may even be valuable for its own sake. Without it our lives are diminished. But no matter how much autonomy we may enjoy at a given time in our lives, it is never secured once and for all. The best our parents can do is prepare us to cope with change and the anti-autonomous forces in the world by building up our powers of self-governance. But without the crucial social and physical contexts to foster their ongoing exercise, these powers will become blunted or distorted.

What's especially insidious about this is that we usually don't notice when or why we are functioning less autonomously. Who among us recognizes the erosion of autonomy which results from a weakened self-image, loss of privacy, or disembodying architecture? The influences are ubiquitous—sometimes subtle (like advertising or architecture) and sometimes more obvious (like domineering parents or surveillance monitoring). Assessing the status of autonomy is fundamental to an intelligent evaluation of society's practices and institutions: the relations and interactions between nurse-patient-doctor-family; teacher-student-parent; employer-employee; government official and citizen. There is so much to tackle, just in terms of autonomy.

You have seen the book move from the more general and basic analyses of autonomy and respect, to the specific interaction of lying and the parent-child relationship, to the private and public contexts for autonomy. These topics inform a host of moral and institutional decisions. For example, how far considerations of respect and privacy ought to limit employee testing—drug, genetic, personality, or lie-detection. To what extent should children's well-being, including autonomy, constrain parental rights. How much control should citizens and consumers have over public space and building. In this last arena, we tend to overlook how members of society can participate in the design of hospitals, schools, libraries, and parks. The autonomy they exercise initially in determining the building's design can be responsible for their subsequent autonomous functioning when using the facility.

Many of the topics covered here, such as architecture, lying, and the parent-child relationship, are rarely examined in light of autonomy in this depth, if at all. Most of the detailed discussions of autonomy, such as Gerald Dworkin's and Lawrence Haworth's, emphasize the significance of autonomy for abstract moral theory or legal/political rights and institutions. By taking up the connections between autonomy and social interaction, I hoped to clarify both. Autonomy should be understood more fully by virtue of drawing out its personal and social implications. And the texture of our social relations should be illuminated by seeing the pivotal role of autonomy in them. The question of how autonomously we function pervades every domain of our lives, from family to work, from where we live to how we think. Perhaps by noting its place in just a few of the lived contexts highlighted here, the importance of autonomy in other areas of our lives will become more apparent.

Notes

Introduction

1. Lawrence Haworth, *Autonomy* (New Haven: Yale University Press, 1986), p. 131.

2. Ibid., p. 207.

Chapter One

1. Robert Benson, "Who is the Autonomous Man, in *The Virtues,* (Belmont, California: Wadsworth, 1987), Kruschwitz and Roberts, eds., p. 207.

2. John Dewey, *Human Nature and Conduct,* (New York: Modern Library, 1957), p. 113.

3. Benson, p. 205.

4. Stanley Benn, "Freedom, Autonomy and the Concept of a Person," *Proceedings of the Aristotelian Society,* Vol. LXXVI (1976), p. 115.

5. Ibid., p. 111.

6. Ibid., p. 113.

7. Robert Ladenson, "A Theory of Personal Autonomy," *Ethics,* 86, 1975, p. 44.

8. Robert C. Roberts, "Will Power and the Virtues," in *The Virtues,* p. 128.

9. I don't mean to slight the distinction between deliberateness and deliberation. To do something deliberately is to do it slowly, unhurriedly. To do something with deliberation, on the other hand, is to reflect about what we are doing; this contrasts with impulsive action, done without thoughtfulness. Perhaps, then, I should be speaking of the "deliberative" will. However, the difference between doing something with deliberation and doing it deliberately applies most clearly to action, not will. When I speak of a "deliberate" will, therefore, obviously I am not referring to the speed with which it takes shape, but rather to a will that is formed through a process of deliberation.

10. Andreas Eshete, "Character, Virtue and Freedom, *Philosophy,* Vol. 57, #222, Oct., p. 498.

11. Harry Frankfurt, "Freedom of the Will and the Concept of a Person," in *Free Will* (Oxford: Oxford University Press, 1982), Gary Watson, ed., p. 88.

12. Eshete, p. 499.

13. N. J. H. Dent, "Desires and Deliberation," in *The Virtues,* p. 109.

14. Ibid., p. 111.

15. Ibid.

16. Eshete, p. 499.

17. Ibid., p. 500.

18. Ibid., p. 497.

19. John Dewey, *Democracy and Education* (New York: Macmillan, 1966), p. 45.

20. John Dewey, *Human Nature and Conduct,* (New York: Modern Library, 1957), p. 207.

21. Dewey develops the notion of decision-making as "dramatic rehearsal" as an alternative to calculation in *Human Nature and Conduct,* Part Three, Sections III and IV ("The Nature of Deliberation," and "Deliberation and Calculation").

22. Benn, p. 124.

23. Ibid., p. 123.

24. Ibid., p. 127.

25. Ibid., p. 127.

26. Gerald Dworkin, "Moral Autonomy," in *Morals, Science and Society*, (Hastings-on-Hudson, New York: The Hastings Center, 1978) Englehardt and Callahan, eds.

27. Gerald Dworkin, "Autonomy and Behavior Control," *Hastings Center Report*, Vol. 6, #1, Feb., p. 24.

28. Dworkin, "Moral Autonomy," p. 169.

29. John Kekes, "Constancy and Purity," *Mind*. 1983, vol. 92, pp. 499–500.

30. Charles Taylor, "Responsibility For Self," in *Free Will*, Watson, p. 124.

31. Dworkin, "Autonomy and Behavior Control."

32. Benn, "Freedom, Autonomy, and the Concept of a Person."

33. Marilyn Friedman emphasizes this in "Autonomy in Social Context," presented at the A.P.A., Pacific Division Meetings, San Francisco, California, March 1987.

34. Frankfurt, p. 86.

35. In fact, if we look carefully at Dworkin's description of authenticity, we see that there is nothing especially moral about it, unless he thinks that the whole enterprise of self-examination is itself a moral one. Frankfurt remarks that a person's second-order volitions do not necessarily manifest a *moral* stance on his part toward his first-order desires. "It may not be from the point of view of morality that the person evaluates his first-order desires," p. 89, ff. 6.

36. See Benn for related but slightly different reasons.

37. Dworkin, "Autonomy and Behavior Control," p. 24.

38. Dworkin actually makes substantive independence an essential component of autonomy. But he does so with misgivings, since, "any notion of commitment (to a lover, a goal, a group) seems to be a denial of substantive independence and hence of autonomy," "Autonomy and Behavior Control," p. 26. I think that my approach can alleviate this difficulty. If the individual can be committed to a cause or person, for example, *without* adopting authoritarian basic (second-order) principles or values, then she can keep the *procedural* independence relevant to autonomy. By analyzing substantive

dependence in terms of the nature of the second-order principles, we can avoid Dworkin's unhappy conclusion that autonomy rules out commitment.

Chapter Two

1. I am glossing over important connections between character and autonomy. For example, the virtue of discipline is needed for the exercise of autonomy. And autonomy itself may be needed for the individual to arrive at a conception of virtuous character or put one's virtues into practice. B.J. Diggs makes the astute observation that the *disposition* to act respectfully is itself a virtue, the virtue of moral sympathy. "A Contractarian View of Respect for Persons," *American Philosophical Quarterly*, Vol. 18, no. 4, Oct. 1981, p. 277.

2. This "unearned respect" is similar to a subclass of what Carl Cranor calls "appraisal respect," in "On Respecting Human Beings as Persons," *Journal of Value Inquiry*, Vol. 17, no. 2, 1983.

3. Kant's conception of free will, upon which his view of moral autonomy rests, involves two senses of will: *Willkur* and *Wille*. *Willkur* is our capability of freedom as spontaneity, the ability to initiate a new causal series. It is freedom *from* direct sensuous necessitation. The freedom of *Willkur* depends on the degree to which it is not determined by the immediate object of desire. It might be thought of as a psychological sense of freedom: the freedom of practical reason to operate rationally with maxims which offer means to the attainment of given ends. Here, reason is still using laws borrowed from nature.

Wille, on the other hand, involves our freedom to give laws for the submission of *Willkur*. The law is itself a *product* of freedom, as reason is itself the source of law—rather than subjecting itself to alien (nature's) law. Freedom in this positive sense is autonomy. It refers to our legislative rather than executive capacity (which is denoted by *Willkur*). The two are, or can be, related. When *Willkur* obeys a law not because of its content (as in hypothetical imperatives), but because of the universal form given by *Wille*, then it is autonomous as well as spontaneous. Thus, *Wille* provides a moral determination of *Willkur* when our ability to act on a principle of reason is informed by the moral law rather than a mere hypothetical imperative. See Lewis White Beck's, *A Commentary* on Kant's Critique of Practical Reason (Chicago: University of Chicago Press, 1960), especially pp. 176–81.

4. R.S. Peters, "Respect For Persons and Fraternity," in *Right and Wrong* (Basic Readings in Ethics), (San Diego: Harcourt, Brace Jovanovich, 1986), Christine Sommers and Robert Fogelin, eds., p. 45.

5. This is why Kant can, indeed must, maintain that material factors do not affect our duty. Apparent influences such as threats and coercion cannot mitigate the moral injunction against lying, for example, because our autonomy qua moral legislative power is in no wise jeopardized by them. Just as the individual's subjective desires are not germane to the moral dictates of self-determined law (save as their *object* in the case of imperfect duties), so are external conditions irrelevant, whether material or social.

6. Lawrence Haworth, *Autonomy* (New Haven: Yale, 1986), p. 191.

7. The perfecting of various abilities is a combination of processes. For instance, language-acquisition in humans is a natural tendency, but which language is spoken and whether it is spoken grammatically is a matter of both developing a natural disposition *and* learning.

8. Haworth, p. 192.

9. Haworth cites a number of developmental psychologists' findings in support of the notion that children are disposed toward and take joy in competence-acquisition. Among those cited are: Harlow, Harlow, and Meyer 1950, "Learning Motivated by a Manipulation Drive," *Journal of Experimental Psychology,* 40:228–34; Kagan and Berkun 1954, "The Reward Value of Running Activity," *Journal of Comparative and Physiological Psychology* 47:108; Loevinger 1976, "Origins of Conscience", *Psychological Issues* 9:265–97; Angyal 1941, *Foundations for a Science of Personality* (New York: Commonwealth Fund).

10. John Stuart Mill, *On Liberty* (Indianapolis: Hackett, 1978), see especially pp. 55–58.

11. As Haworth convincingly argues, however, this good does not attach simply to acting with liberty, but rather requires autonomous action. See Haworth, chapters 7–9.

12. This account obviously excludes nature and dead people as proper objects of respect. Ordinary language use can be accounted for, however, by the connection between nature or the dead and autonomous beings. For example, we have an obligation to take care of nature ("treat it with respect") because of the interests of present and future autonomous beings. Respect for these people, then, demands certain behavior of us toward nature. In addition to this sort of consideration, we speak colloquially of respecting the dead for the added reasons of the symbolic connection between the corpse and the once living moral agent, as well as because of the possible impact desecrating behavior could have on our own character.

There are other moral attitudes and responses, besides respect, which are demanded of us and some of them extend to non-autonomous beings. Pity, care, affection, tolerance, patience, kindness, and appreciation, for instance, should be shown beings not entitled to respect as well as those that are.

13. Considerations of utility, justice, virtue, as well as special obligations resulting from promises, relationships, and the like are distinct from respect. However, they may be related to it. The idea that utilities should be justly distributed, for example, would seem to depend on the belief that each is entitled—out of respect—to be treated as an equal. The recipient of a promise, moreover, must be an autonomous being, capable of understanding such language and governing his affairs in light of it.

14. B. J. Diggs, p. 276.

15. George Nakhnikian, "Love in Human Reason," *Midwest Studies in Philosophy,* Vol. III, 1978, p. 296.

16. Bernard Williams, "The Idea of Equality," in *Philosophy, Politics and Society* (Second Series) (Oxford: Blackwell, 1962), Laslett and Runciman, eds., pp. 110–131.

R. S. Peters voices a similar view: " 'Respect for persons' is therefore a principle which summarizes the attitude which we must adopt towards others with whom we are prepared seriously to discuss what ought to be done. Their point of view must be taken into account as sources of claims and interests" (p. 50).

17. Onora O'Neill, "Between Consenting Adults," *Philosophy and Public Affairs,* Summer 1985, Vol. 14, no. 3, p. 271.

18. Diggs, p. 277.

19. John Rawls, *A Theory of Justice* (Cambridge, Mass.: Harvard University Press, 1971), p. 337.

20. Robert Arrington, "On Respect," *Journal of Value Inquiry*, Vol. XII, No. 1, Spring 1978, p. 4. Arrington also sees the following flaw in the Williams' position:

> Adopting the human view can be, in addition to a source of respect, also the means of treating a man in some highly disrespectful and degrading ways. It is doubtful that there would be such things as cruelty and torture unless someone adopted the human view—thereby looking upon his victim as a person with feelings, hopes, and intentions—and then proceeded to exploit the knowledge gained in this way (pp. 2–3).

Williams's notion of the "human view," therefore, may be necessary but is not sufficient to treating people with respect.

21. Arrington, p. 5.

22. Arrington, p. 8, my italics.

23. Nakhnikian, p. 297. In light of the traditional Kantian meaning of "autonomy," it may sound strange to claim dependency rather than heteronomy as the opposite of autonomy. The oddness should be dispelled by recalling that Kant conceives autonomy narrowly, in terms of motivation and only for the sake of morally worthy action or will. Kant doesn't object to heteronomy in most spheres of life, since acting on one's desires or interests in non-moral matters is what most of life is all about. Interestingly enough, though, there *is* a way in which dependency (as here understood) is heteronomous in Kant's sense: to rely excessively on others is to let one's will be determined by something other than one's own rationality.

24. Nakhnikian, p. 300. He has in mind the aspects of growth and well-being "that cannot be affected except insofar as [the individual] is willing to use" his own powers (p. 297).

25. Thomas Hill, "Servility and Self-Respect," in *Today's Moral Problems* (New York: Macmillan, 1979), 2nd ed., Richard Wasserstrom, ed., p. 138. Hill's own view is that moral rights are the basis of respect, including self-respect. This is not the place to argue against this view, but I will note two things in passing.

Showing respect for many if not all rights *amounts* to showing respect for autonomy. In addition, autonomy is a plausible basis for possessing rights.

26. Arrington, p. 11.

27. See Hugo Adam Bedeau, "Egalitarianism and the Ideal of Equality," in *Equality* (New York: Atherton, 1967), J. R. Pennock and J. W. Chapman, eds., pp. 3–27.

28. Such considerations also raise questions concerning the retarded. First it should be noted that the term "retarded" covers an enormous range of intellectual and autonomous functioning, from those quite competent to control their own lives (mildly retarded), to those totally helpless (severe and profound). The argument offered here dictates that autonomy be encouraged to whatever degree achievable, and that responsibilities be granted in proportion to the level of autonomous functioning achieved.

In addition, the severely and profoundly retarded cannot be suitable objects of respect since so deeply devoid of autonomy. They are, however, suitable objects of loving care. Whether they have a "right" to such treatment is another question, one which Jeffrie Murphy, for example, answers in the affirmative, from a Rawlsian perspective ("Rights and Borderline Cases," in *Ethics and Mental Retardation* (Dordrecht: D. Reidel, Pub., 1984), Kopelman and Moskop, eds., pp. 3–17). The point here is simply that lacking the status to be treated with respect is hardly the last word in what the severely retarded are entitled to, or more generally put, how we "ought" to treat them.

We might also note an important difference between animals and the severely retarded. Neither are autonomous, but where most animals can get along quite well, often better, without interferences by those of us who are autonomous, the severely retarded are dependent upon us for survival and comfort. This, too, might impose obligations upon us, especially since some of us are causally and morally responsible for their existence in the world.

29. There might well be other reasons for our obligation to foster autonomy in children or others. Utilitarian considerations for the individual's and society's welfare, for instance, seem to argue convincingly for it. Autonomy is needed for happiness, both as ingredient in and instrumental to the individual's happiness. Autonomous activity not only makes up a part of a person's welfare, but is instrumentally needed for him to do what only he can do

to secure certain benefits for himself. To fail to promote a child's autonomy, then, is to jeopardize his welfare. Of course, not all adults are equally placed to effect a child's development. Family and teachers, for instance, have a greater responsibility in the development of autonomy (see Chapter Four), but all adults have an obligation at least not to hinder this development. In addition, it is plausible to think that self-governing people are less of a burden to others, individually and as a society, than those unable to control their own lives. Autonomous individuals, moreover, probably can contribute more to society's overall welfare.

30. Although distinct, the potential for autonomy and the potential for life both raise the issue of our obligation to help realize an organism's potential for some good. For an insightful discussion of the "potentiality principle" as it applies to the potential for life, see R.M. Hare's "Abortion and the Golden Rule," *Philosophy and Public Affairs*, Vol. 4, no. 3, Spring, 1975.

Alison Jaggar offers the plausible thesis that "The right to life . . . means the right to a full human life and to whatever means are necessary to achieve this" ("Abortion and a Woman's Right to Decide," in *Women and Philosophy* (New York: Capricorn Books, 1976), Carol Gould and Marx Wartofsky, eds., p. 351). If this is on the right track and I am correct in claiming that autonomy is necessary for happiness (or a "full human life"), then the right to life would entail the child's right to develop as autonomously as circumstances allow.

Chapter Three

1. See Sisslea Bok, *Lying: Moral Choice in Public and Private Life* (New York: Random House, 1978), p. 32. This is akin to Arnold Isenberg's "constancy principle," which holds that what is inherently bad in any lie is the same for all, constant from one lie to the next. "Deontology and the Ethics of Lying," in *Aesthetics and the Theory of Criticism; Selected Essays of Arnold Isenberg*, ed. William Callhan (Chicago: University of Chicago Press, 1973).

2. Roderick Chisholm and Thomas D. Feehan (in "The Intent to Deceive," *Journal of Philosophy*, Vol. 74, no. 3 (March 1977), pp. 143–59) offer a helpful, albeit technically elaborate definition, a summary of which follows.

An individual *lies* when he *asserts* a propositon to another which
he believes to be not true or false; he *asserts* a proposition when
he *states* it under conditions which he believes justify the other in
believing that he (the liar) intends to contribute causally to the
other's believing that he (the liar) accepts the proposition; he *states*
a proposition when he believes that the expression he utters has
the standard use in the language of expressing this proposition and
he thereby intends the other to believe that he (the liar) intends
to utters the expression in this way.
The authors also fruitfully distinguish between deception by
commission and deception by omission.

    3. It is interesting to see what happens to my position in the
case of unsuccessful lies, but we should keep in mind the specific
bases of failure. If the failure is due to the would-be deceived not
believing the false statement, then the first inherent disvalue
(restriction of the deceived's autonomy) is reversed. The attempted
lie backfires on the liar and *he* loses autonomy due to lack of trust
just as he would when an initially successful lie is eventually
"uncovered." The second inherent disvalue (self-opposition) still
obtains, but briefly. Because the would-be deceived does not believe
the statement, the opposition between what the liar says and
believes dissipates, to be replaced, perhaps, by negative self-
appraisal such as shame.

    If the failure is due to the statement being true, again, the
first inherent disvalue is reversed. The would-be deceived carries
on believing a true statement. The "liar" however has two false
beliefs: one concerning the content of the statement, the other the
would-be deceived's beliefs. Now, of course, the liar is no worse off
after the lie with regard to the content of the conveyed belief; he
thought it false before the lie and still does. But, believing that
the would-be deceived now possesses a false belief could rather
easily restrict the liar's autonomy. The liar has become his own
deceived due to the truthfulness of the statement. The second
inherent disvalue obtains since there is still opposition between
what the liar believes and what he says.

    Whether the contingent dangers are still risked is, of course,
another question. If the "deceived" is not taken in by the lie,
perhaps the liar risks self-loathing or resentment of the deceived
(for not being an easy mark) rather than loss of respect for the
deceived. If the statement is indeed true, maybe the liar risks lack
of integration of his beliefs as well as lack of self-knowledge. He
will still conceal his real beliefs and be deprived of the benefits of

open discussion for both integration of beliefs and self-knowledge. The details of this brief tangential discussion should be clarified by the subsequent examination of the two inherent disvalues and their risks to the liar.

4. S. I. Benn and W. L. Weinstein, "Being Free to Act and Being a Free Man," *Mind*, Vol. 80, no. 318 (April 1971), p. 197.

5. Benn and Weinstein, p. 210. The fact that practical wisdom may be needed to decide whom to trust suggests that we are sometimes responsible for being duped, but that is another issue (see chapter 1, first section).

6. I am using the word simply to distinguish the one who lies from the deceived or other parties. Strictly speaking, only those habituated to lying are properly considered "liars."

7. Isenberg, p. 260.

8. Contrary to some philosophers, such as Sissela Bok, I see an important difference between excusing and justifying actions (including lies). We excuse the *person* for committing the act; he is exonerated because of circumstances or some state he is in. Being misinformed about a danger, for example, might excuse someone for lying. But the fact that the lie occurred is nevertheless lamentable or unfortunate. The *act* is still wrong and is excused *after* the fact.

On the other hand, we *justify* an *action*: after *and* before its performance. Circumstances or relationships make morally permissible what might otherwise be prohibited. Lying might be justified, for instance, by the deceived's manifest intentions to do harm. The act is not wrong, though we might decry the circumstances which permit it.

The distinction between excuses and justifications will be developed specifically in connection with the way lying restricts autonomy.

9. I do not mean to suggest that white lies are the only or main cases of excused lies. But their frequency and demarcated "classification" make them compelling examples. A *serious* lie could, of course, be excused, for example because of an excusable error on the part of the liar.

10. It is because Kant has an abstract view of freedom, unindividuated and unaffected by concrete conditions, that his strictures on lying (among other practices) cannot take coercion

into account. Yet coercion provides just the sort of cases which make his moral conclusions seem counterintuitive.

11. In deontological language, the unjustified threat to my autonomy mitigates my "prima facie" duty not to lie or the presumption of such a duty. Prima facie or presumptive duties are the deontologist's formulation of prohibitions which may be overridden in particular cases. The deontologist, however, bases duty on the concept of autonomy or freedom. Autonomy is the ground of duty. Therefore, the jeopardization of autonomy is not on a par with other considerations of duty. Autonomy reaches "deeper" than any particular duty, such as not to lie, since it grounds them all. Thus, defending my freedom is not on the same moral level with my particular duty not to lie. It takes precedence over such particular duties.

12. Charles Fried, *Right and Wrong* (Cambridge, Mass.: Harvard University Press, 1978), p. 68.

13. An example of non-lying linguistic deception might be helpful. Suppose that I am asked whether I expect to attend a meeting tomorrow and I reply, "No, I'm leaving for Chicago tomorrow." Although I *am* leaving for Chicago tomorrow, my departure in no way interferes with attending the meeting; I could easily do both. The questioner quite reasonably and simply "fills in" that the departure would interfere with attending the meeting and infers the false belief that the attendance is impossible *because* I am leaving town. He takes me to be offering a *reason* when I have only laid the statement about leaving town *alongside* my negative response.

It might be, however, that this and all other non-lying linguistic deception can plausibly be analyzed as an implicit or eliptical lie in which the deceived reasonably fills in the false belief (which the liar never explicitly states). Thus, in the above example, the deceived questioner infers that I won't be attending the meeting *because* I will be on my way to Chicago. On this analysis of non-lying linguistic deception, it escapes the label "lie" on a "mere technicality"—a difference without much difference. If cogent, we should not chafe at the lack of a strong basis for differentiating the sub-species of lies from linguistic deception as a whole.

14. Chisholm and Feehan, p. 153.

15. If lying shows greater disrespect than other forms of deception (including non-lying linguistic deception), then it should

follow from my position that lying has a greater tendency to engender disrespect as a character trait, or a tendency to engender a greater degree of disrespect.

16. Isenberg, p. 262.

17. Isenberg, p. 260. Now suppression in general is not a constructive way to reestablish psychic order when we face a dilemma or try to resolve conflict. It is not a genuine harmonization of the opposed internal factions. In the case of lying, the body appears to give isomorphic evidence of the psychological rift occasioned by suppression. Changes in the electrical conductivity of the skin, increase in heart rate and breathing indicate a somatic playing out of the more subtle psychological conflict.

18. Isenberg, p. 261. Saying something *other* than what we believe, however, *need* not call for reason or explanation. Specific contexts, such as joking, drama, debate and the like carry with them such reasons and so they are not usually "called for" except by or for the uninitiated.

19. Immanual Kant, *Doctrine of Virtue*, p. 428.

20. There is an obvious irony in the liar's restriction of the deceived's autonomy; the liar stands a good chance of losing more autonomy for himself in the long run. Perhaps not so obvious is the fact that such irony is not merely an accidental feature of lying. Irony always involves the juxtaposition of opposites (only when Jones finally stops trying for a promotion, for instance, does he get one). Ironic situations involve opposition: between past and present; desire and action; thought and deed; and so forth. Practices in which opposition is a defining feature, then, especially lend themselves to the creation of irony. It should not be surprising that lying helps produce irony to the extend that is does since in lying we say the opposite of what we believe. The opposition of lying is conducive to a variety of ironies.

21. This yields another, somewhat perverse irony. Once sufficiently out of touch with his real beliefs, the liar is no longer *technically* lying since he believes what he asserts to be true (the "natural transition" from belief to speech totally corrupted). This pathological state, of course, confirms rather than weakens my claim concerning the danger posed by lying to self-knowledge. A pathological liar of the sort just mentioned is losing self-knowledge of the most profound sort. The tension between what is believed

and what is said appears to have dissolved. He has come to believe what he once knew to be intended falsehoods. We might be tempted to think of this as a *new* self to be identified with the new set of beliefs. But this seems wrong-headed. If pressed, the "convinced liar" would discover himself confused over what he *really* believed since the hitherto "lies" would not jibe with other of his beliefs.

22. The situation, thus, *also* determines the degree to which the self-opposition created by the lie is *perpetuated*. Lies in general create a self-perpetuating opposition between thought and speech because the former must be concealed. Contrast this with opposition in thought which is not self-perpetuating (because not self-enclosing): we pose an objection to our own thesis or deliberate over competing lines of action. In such cases there is a lack of integration of opinion but it is not located within a mechanism for perpetuation or exacerbation.

23. I am indebted to Robert Audi for his "Iago" objections to a paper on this subject which was presented at the Western Division Meetings of the APA in Detroit, in Spring 1980.

Chapter Four

1. In the case of adoptive parents, of course, those who are assuming the job of rearing the child are exercising autonomy in making this choice. Once again, then, autonomy enters as a precondition for having basic obligations.

2. Joel Feinberg, "The Child's Right to an Open Future," in *Whose Child? Children's Rights, Parental Authority and State Power*, ed. by Aiken and LaFollette (Totawa, N.J.: Rowman and Littlefield, 1980), p. 126.

3. Marilyn Friedman, "Friendship and Moral Growth," presented at the Central Division Meetings, A.P.A., May 1987.

4. Lawrence Haworth, *Autonomy* (New Haven: Yale, 1986), p. 123.

5. Elizabeth Newson, "Unreasonable Care: the establishment of selfhood," in *Human Values*, ed., Godfrey Vesey (Sussex, England: Harvester Press, 1978), p. 2.

6. Daniel Callahan, "What Do Children Owe Elderly Parents?" *Hastings Center Report*, Vol. 15, No. 2, April 1985, p. 35.

7. This is not to say, however, that enjoying unrefusable benefits never creates *some* sort of obligation. In some cases, such as those involving natural resources, we may be obliged not to waste the benefit. In others, such as innocently enjoying stolen goods, we may be obliged to return what's left or make restitution. But these are not cases of *reciprocal* obligation.

8. Jane English, "What Do Grown Children Owe Their Parents?", in *Morality and Moral Controversies* (New Jersey: Prentice-Hall, 1981), John Arthur, ed., p. 149. English' contention that obligations between friends are *only* mutual, never reciprocal, need not occupy us here. I have indirectly argued against this at the end of the second section (Reciprocal Obligations).

9. A Kantian approach to the relationship between love and the behavior it motivates might help explain why love and certain behavior are so "naturally" connected in our thinking. Love, by its very definition, necessarily motivates caring behavior where feasible (the behavior we might think it obliges us to engage in). This is because to will an end is to will the means to its achievement. Kant offers this as an explication of simply what it *is* or means to will an end, in contrast, say, to merely wish for it. To love another is to will her welfare. To will her welfare is to will the behavior, within limits, which will help bring it about. Therefore, to love another is to will helping behavior. From this it follows that someone who didn't provide reasonable help to one he claimed to love really didn't love this other person. To love is necessarily to be moved to act in helping ways just as to will a technical end, such as musical accomplishment, is to will the relevant means to its achievement (practicing).

10. Callahan, pp. 35–36.

11. Of course, this specification of our general obligation is hardly confined to parents and children; similar opportunities for fulfilling general obligations might present themselves in other relationships.

12. Jane English, for example.

13. Although "parents" includes guardians and adoptive parents, in what follows I shall be taking those who are, in addition, the biological parents as the paradigm. Genetic similarity makes a slightly stronger case for some of my claims.

14. I will explicitly refer to "adult" (or "grown") child and "young" child where age is relevant. Where the relationship or status is what matters "child" *simpliciter* will be used.

15. There may, of course, be other obstacles to parent-adult child friendship, such as gender-linked roles, sexism, or agism. But these make no difference to my thesis. My claim is meant to hold in the best of circumstances, in which sexism, for instance, plays no part in the family dynamic.

Similarly, there are many other significant features of both complete friendship and the ideal parent-adult child relationship which have been put to one side for the purposes of this discussion.

16. This refers to the virtuous or "true" friendship. In the friendships of utility and pleasure, the type of good received need not be the same, but must be proportional or there is a lack of sufficient motivation for the friendship, at least on one side.

17. See Laurence Thomas' "Friendship," *Synthese*, Vol. 72, 1987, for a helpful discussion of the importance of self-disclosure and trust in friendship.

18. A body of social theory and empirical findings supports the view that self-concept has a significant bearing on the amount of autonomy exercised by the individual. See, for example, Piaget's *The Moral Judgment of the Child* (New York: Basic Books, 1966) and Victor Tausk's "On the Origin of the 'Influencing Machine' in Schizophrenia," *Psychoanalytic Quarterly* 1933, 2, 519–556.

Studies of people who are systematically, chronically denied privacy, for example, find deterioration in their autonomy as a result of erosion of self-concept. The connection between privacy, self-concept, and autonomy is developed and examined in chapter 5, on privacy.

19. While the nature and details of our self-concept affect how autonomously we function, these specific examples have little to do with the autonomy we exhibit in *particular* relationships, such as the relationship with our parents.

20. Laurence Thomas makes a similar point about the way the parent's authority over the young child carries over into the parent-adult child relationship, preventing friendship. Thomas confines his thoughtful discussion of parental authority to the moral variety (primarily in terms of parents being *entitled* to make assessments of their children rather than, say, being moral models). He doesn't

explore the de facto authority (power) which seems as important an obstacle to complete friendship between parents and their grown children.

21. Similar relations may hold between siblings, other relatives, or childhood friends who continue to see each other as adults. I suspect that, as with parents and children, loving siblings can't quite be friends (but will experience values missing from friendship). This is an interesting but distinct area of inquiry.

22. Recall Marilyn Friedman, who suggests that friends can facilitate our moral autonomy by providing a different standpoint, "from which to assess one's choices, one's values and principles, one's very character." Increase in diversity of perspectives from which to judge rules, values, and character yields increase in autonomy. If Friedman is correct, then friends may be in a position to enhance our autonomy in ways that parents, because of the familiarity of their convictions and values, cannot.

23. The way parents boast about their children (whether young or adult) attests to this prideful identification. Parental boasting appears to be about the children and not the parents themselves. However, when parents violate the conventional limits on how much bragging is acceptable, their immodesty is exposed. They are seen as praising themselves in their children.

24. The relationship between parents and their grown children may possess another value based on the resemblance which contributes to their mutual identification. The resemblence affords a unique context for self-knowledge and self-improvement. Because they can see so much of themselves in each other, parents and adult children to some extent hold a mirror up to one another. We are able to discover both virtues and flaws, potentials and deficiencies by interacting with our parents and children.

No doubt we also gain self-knowledge by being with those who are different, such as friends. This is a complementary way of learning about ourselves. Moreover, while we *might* also see ourselves in other people, resemblance to them is not structurally part of the relationship. The sense of being confronted with portions of ourselves in another is built into the fabric of the parent-adult child relationship and is a source of added value. Perhaps it isn't the self-knowledge which is so valuable, but the *way* we come to acquire it.

Seeing flaws in ourselves by virture of recognizing ourselves in our parents, for instance, may provide a unique impetus for self-improvement. To see ourselves externalized in another gives a kind of concreteness to beliefs about ourselves. Because of the "solidity" of confronting something we don't like in ourselves in the person of another, we resolve to change ourselves. So, too, might we also see potential in ourselves for developing laudable traits by means of recognizing resemblances with our parents. In the best cases, then, we don't merely see ourselves in our parents, but we take the discovery of resemblance as a propadeutic to self-improvement.

25. The sort of unconditional love I ascribe to parents is similar to, but different from agape or "neighbor" love. It is similar to it in that both are independent of the person's characteristics or accomplishments and neither depends on what the person does for the one who loves. Both kinds of love, therefore, "accept" the individual for who he or she is. They differ in that parental love, as indicated, is based on the particular relationship; agape abstracts from any such relationship. Much more could and should be said on this than is appropriate here.

26. Our relation to each is, in turn, mediated by our connection with the other. We are no logner simply our parents' child when we have a child of our own. Our understanding and appreciation of parents are deepened by rearing our own child. Similarly does the relationship with our parents condition the interaction we enjoy with our own child.

Chapter Five

1. Stanley I. Benn, "Privacy, Freedom, and Respect for Persons," in *Privacy* (New York: Atherton Press, 1971), J. Roland Pennock and John Chapman, eds., pp. 10–11.

Benn's argument for the importance of privacy reverses its relationship to autonomy. Where *I* argue that privacy is needed for the development and continuance of autonomy, Benn sees autonomy as the moral basis for granting people privacy. Autonomous people deserve respect and granting privacy shows respect. I think that Benn's account has serious difficulties. He claims that when we secretly deprive someone of privacy, "he is wronged because the significance to him of his enterprise, assumed unobserved, is deliberately falsified [by the observer]" (p. 11).

But *why* does spying on someone falsify the *significance* of his enterprise, or his self worth? Perhaps because such spying implicitly says that this (or you) aren't worthy of my abstaining and consideraton. But then we still need to know *why* granting privacy in fact does this, shows respect for autonomy. As Benn acknowledges, it has to be more than refraining from violating the individual's wishes. The view I argue for here is that we show people respect as autonomous beings by granting them privacy because privacy is a *condition* for the development and exercise of autonomy.

2. Jeffrey H. Reiman, "Privacy, Intimacy, and Personhood," in *Today's Moral Problems* (New York: Macmillan, 1979), 2nd ed., Richard Wasserstrom, ed., p. 387.

3. Robert Sommer, *Personal Space: The Behavioral Basis of Design* (Englewood Cliffs, N.J.: Prentice-Hall, 1969), pp. 68–69.

4. Richard B. Parker, "Privacy," in *Readings in Philosophy of Law* (Englewood Cliffs, New Jersey: Prentice-Hall, 1984), John Arthur and William Shaw, eds., pp. 602–03.

5. Thomas Scanlon, "Thomson on Privacy," *Philosophy and Public Affairs*, Vol. 4, No. 4 (Summer 1975), p. 315.

6. Reiman, p. 380.

7. Such empirical support would require operationalizing the concept of autonomy and then finding that decreases in it depend upon loss of privacy. Of course, this would also require subsidiary hypotheses concerning levels of privacy, duration of privacy deprivation, and the nature of the social conditions. It might turn out, for example, that the degree of privacy needed for the development and maintenance of autonomy is directly proportional to such social features as intolerance or oppression. People may be able to develop rich self-concepts and hence autonomy with *little* privacy when the risks of self-expression, self-exposure, and deviance are minimal.

8. These and other considerations would have to be brought to bear on the counter-claim that children raised without much privacy, for example, on a Kibbutz, nevertheless exhibit considerable autonomy. Aside from determining exactly what constitutes lack of privacy, the counter-claim faces evidence which actually indicates lack of autonomy development. In *Children of the Kibbutz*, Melford E. Spiro offers a critical analysis of the personality of the "Sabras"—Kibbutz-raised children. Among the salient personality traits found to characterize the Sabras are

introversion, insecurity, and hostility feelings. Such traits, especially insecurity, at least *suggest* limited autonomy. It is difficult to assess the impact of lack of privacy since other aspects of the environment could also be causal factors in the development of autonomy or its lack. Limitations on family interaction and lack of private property, as well as the ideological and political realities of Kibbutz life could all play a role.

9. Charles Fried, "Privacy: A Rational Context," in *Today's Moral Problems*, p. 368.

10. Isaiah Berlin, *Four Essays on Liberty* (Oxford: Oxford University Press, 1969), p. 124.

11. Mary Mothersill, "Educating the Imagination," in *Human Values* (Sussex, U. K.: Harvester Press, 1978), Godfrey Vesey, ed., pp. 59–60.

12. Ibid., p. 59.

13. R. Laufer, H. Proshansky, and M. Wolfe, "Some Analytic Dimensions of Privacy," in *Environmental Psychology* (New York: Holt, Rinehart, and Winston, 1976), 2nd ed., H. Proshansky, W. Ittelson, and L. Rivlin, eds., p. 206.

14. R. S. Peters, "Respect for Persons and Fraternity," in *Right and Wrong* (San Diego: Harcourt, Brace, Jovanovich, 1986), Christina Hoff Sommers, ed., pp. 46–47.

15. See, for example, Piaget's *The Moral Judgment of the Child* (New York: Basic Books, 1966) and Tausk's "On the Origin of the 'Influencing Machine' in Schizophrenia," *Psychoanalytic Quarterly*, 1933, 2, 519–556.

16. Erving Goffman, *Asylums* (New York: Anchor Books, 1961), p. 23, my italics.

17. W. Ittelson, H. Proshansky, and L. Rivlin, "The Environmental Psychology of the Psychiatric Ward," in *Environmental Psychology* (New York: Holt, Rinehart, and Winston, 1967), 1st ed., H. Proshansky, W. Ittelson, and L. Rivlin, eds., p. 438.

18. P. Sivadon, "Space as Experienced: Therapeutic Implications," in *Environmental Psychology*, 1st ed., p. 414.

19. Hyman Gross, "Privacy and Autonomy," in *Philosophy of Law* (Encino, California: Dickenson, 1975), Joel Feinberg and Hyman Gross, eds., p. 191.

20. Charles Taylor, "Responsibility for Self," in *Free Will* (Oxford: Oxford University Press, 1982), Gary Watson, ed., p. 111.

21. Ibid., p. 126.

22. Ibid., p. 124.

23. Adina Schwartz, "Meaningful Work," *Ethics*, Vol. 92, July 1982, p. 638.

24. Laurence tribe, *American Constitutional Law* (Mineola, New York: The Foundation Press, 1978), p. 966.

25. Arnold Simmel, "Privacy is not an Isolated Freedom," in *Privacy*, p. 73.

26. Barry Schwartz, "The Social Psychology of Privacy," *American Journal of Sociology*, Vol. 73, May 1968, p. 747.

27. By "surveillance," I have in mind the situation in which an individual is under relatively uninterrupted observation or monitoring. It implies singleness of agency—if not in person, then purpose. If five people see me now and five others an hour later, that is not surveillance, so long as the two groups are not in cahoots. Moreover, to the extent that I have some control over when, where, and who sees me, as in my choosing to go out for a walk, to that extent, surveillance does not obtain.

28. Fried, p. 370.

29. Simmel, p. 80.

30. Alan P. Bates, "Privacy—A Useful Concept?" *Social Forces*, Vol. 42, May 1964, pp. 432–33.

31. Benn, p. 26.

32. Ibid., p. 10.

33. Michael A. Weinstein, "The Uses of Privacy in the Good Life," in *Privacy*, p. 103.

34. Edgar Z. Friedberg, *Coming of Age in America* (New York: Random House, 1963), p. 291.

35. Hannah Arendt, in *The Human Condition*, argues that the importance attributed to intimacy is distinctively modern. It stands in contrast, say, to the ancient Greek emphasis on participation in public life. However "relative" to our age and culture, the importance of intimacy to an autonomous self-concept probably spans a fairly broad range of periods and cultures.

36. Fried, p. 369.

37. Jeffrie Murphy points out an interesting analog of Fried's "moral capital" in his discussion of blackmail ("Blackmail: A Preliminary Inquiry," *Monist,* Vol. 63, #2, April 1980). In casting about for what precisely is wrong with blackmail, he considers the idea that the blackmailer is, "turning a portion of a person's life into an economic commodity" (p. 25). By itself, Murphy argues, this just will not work because the snoop who sells "news" to the cheap tabloids is also using information about someone as a commodity, and we do not find this objectionable (at least not in the same way or degree as we find blackmail). What is interesting to us, here, however, is the way personal information functions as a social commodity, on Fried's view, and as a genuinely economic commodity, on at least a preliminary examination of blackmail. If our misgivings about blackmail have some foundation in the commoditization of a person's life, then perhaps we should be wary of Fried's analogous commoditization. The blackmail parallel seems to lend support to Reiman's complaint that Fried's view, "Suggests a market conception of personal intimacy," p. 382.

38. Reiman, p. 383.

39. Simmel, p. 81.

Chapter Six

1. H. Allen Brooks, "Wright and the Destruction of the Box," in *Writing on Wright* (Cambridge, Mass.: M.I.T. Press, 1981), Brooks, ed., p. 177.

2. William H. Whyte, *The Social Life of Small Urban Spaces,* (Washington, D.C.: The Conservation Foundation, 1980), p. 34.

3. Ibid., p. 35.

4. Ibid., p. 28.

5. Robert Sommer, "Going Outdoors for Study Space," *Landscape Architecture,* LVIII, No. 3 (1968), pp. 196–98.

6. Kevin Lynch, *The Image of the City* (Cambridge, Mass.: M.I.T. and Harvard University Press, 1960).

7. Kiyoshi Izumi, "Psychosocial Phenomena and Building Design," *Building Research,* 1965, Vol. 2, p. 10.

8. Paul Sivadon, "Space as Experienced: Therapeutic Implications," in *Environmental Psychology* (New York: Holt, Rinehart, and Winston, 1967) 1st ed., H. Proshansky, W. Ittelson, and L. Rivlin, eds., p. 416.

9. Joan Didion, "Many Mansions," *The White Album* (New York: Simon and Schuster, 1979), p. 69.

10. Robert Venturi, *Complexity And Contradiction* (New York: Museum of Modern Art, 1966), p. 129.

11. Venturi, p. 130. It is ironic that what Venturi gives to the creation of a community by way of strengthening autonomy, he takes away by weakening the social. He takes the fact that "Americans feel uncomfortable sitting in a square," as a basis for rejecting the open piazza or square as ever appropriate for contemporary American cities. Rather than congregate in a piazza (traditionally designed, he acknowledges, for *collective* as well as individual use), Americans "should be working at the office or home with the family looking at television," p. 131.

12. Whyte, p. 84.

13. R. L. Berger, "Bodily Experience and Expression of Emotion," quoted by Elaine and Bernard Feder, M. D., "The Theraputic Use of Dance and Movement," in *Helping Through Action—Action-Oriented Therapies* (Amherst, Mass.: Human Resource Development Press, 1982), Nickerson and O'Laughlin, eds., p. 143.

14. Feder and Feder, p. 143.

15. Ibid.

16. J. B. Jackson, *Landscapes* (Amherst, Mass.: University of Massachusetts Press, 1970), Ervin Zube, ed., p. 83.

17. Ibid., p. 84.

18. Sivadon, p. 418.

19. The distinction between "dead" and "living" public space is Richard Sennett's, in *The Fall of Public Man* (New York: Vintage, 1974).

20. Sennett, p. 13.

21. Ibid., p. 14.

22. Jane Jacobs, *The Death and Life of Great American Cities* (New York: Random House, 1961), p. 87, my italics.

23. Sennett, p. 15.

24. William L. Yancey, "Architecture, Interaction, and Social Control: The Case of a Large-Scale Public Housing Project," in *Environmental Psychology* (New York: Holt, Rinehart, and Winston, 1976), 2nd ed., H. Proshansky et. al., eds., p. 456.

25. Yancey, p. 457.

26. Robert Sommer, *Personal Space: The Behavioral Basis of Design* (Englewood Cliffs, N.J.: Prentice-Hall, 1969), p. 100.

27. Jacobs, p. 56.

28. Ibid., p. 57.

29. Ibid., p. 60.

30. Ibid., p. 65.

31. Humphry Osmond, "Function as the Basis of Psychiatric Ward Design," in Proshansky, *Environmental Psychology*, 1st ed., p. 567.

32. Rober Sommer, *Personal Space*, p. 171.

33. I am focusing only on the nature and impact of architectural design. A crucial, larger question concerns the underlying causes of the architecture itself. Architecture is not an independent phenomenon; it reflects prevailing social, economic, and political institutions. It seems plausible to see the concentration of capital and the demands of a market society as playing a major role in the standardization of architecture (as well as many other art forms, commodities, and institutions). Ever increasingly businesses cease to be locally owned, as national and multinational corporations "chain" link the country. The construction companies which build the theatres, ballparks, and malls, are also predominantly national in scope. The threat to individuality posed by placeless architecture, therefore, goes well beyond the purview of this chapter.

34. Brian Neilson, "Dialogue With the City: The Evolution of Baseball Parks," *Landscape*, Vol. 29, No. 1, 1986, p. 41.

35. Ibid., p. 43.

36. Ibid., p. 44.

37. Ibid., p. 42.

38. Whyte, p. 76.

39. William Severini Kowinski, "The Malling of America," *New Times*, Vol. 10, No. 9, May 1, 1978, p. 35.

40. For an insightful discussion of the differences between city-time and nature-time, see John McDermott's "Glass Without Feet," in *Streams of Experience* (Amherst: University of Massachusetts, 1986).

41. John McDermott, "Space, Time, and Touch," in *The Culture of Experience* (New York: New York University, 1976), p. 224.

42. Herbert Marcuse, *An Essay on Liberation* (Boston: Beacon Press, 1969), p. 29.

Index

213